P9-AOV-649

FLORIDA STATE
UNIVERSITY LIBRARIES

JUL 21 1999

TALLAHASSEE, FLORIDA

GARLAND STUDIES IN

THE HISTORY OF AMERICAN LABOR

edited by
STUART BRUCHEY
ALLAN NEVINS PROFESSOR EMERITUS
COLUMBIA UNIVERSITY

A GARLAND SERIES

LABOR STRIFE AND THE ECONOMY IN THE 1970s

A DECADE OF DISCORD

MICHAEL J. KAPSA

GARLAND PUBLISHING, INC.
A MEMBER OF THE TAYLOR & FRANCIS GROUP
NEW YORK & LONDON / 1998

HD
5324
.K28
1998

Copyright © 1998 Michael J. Kapsa
All rights reserved

Library of Congress Cataloging-in-Publication Data

Kapsa, Michael J., 1959–
    Labor strife and the economy in the 1970s : a decade of
discord / Michael J. Kapsa.
        p.   cm. — (Garland studies in the history of American
labor)
    Includes bibliographical references and index.
    ISBN 0-8153-3181-9 (alk. paper)
    1. Strikes and lockouts—United States—History—20th
century. 2. Labor disputes—United States—History—20th century. 3. Industrial relations—United States—History—20th
century. 4. Collective bargaining—United States—History—20th
century. 5. United States—Economic conditions—1971–1981.
I. Title. II. Series.
HD5324.K28 1998
331.892'73'09047—dc21

                                                                98-39720

Printed on acid-free, 250-year-life paper
Manufactured in the United States of America

To
Jeanne

Table of Contents

Foreword

This book is a micro-level analysis of strike activity in U.S. manufacturing for 1971 through 1980. Using a large micro-data sample of U.S. collective bargaining units and strike occurrences initially developed by Cynthia Gramm, the research focuses on the conditions surrounding the breakdown of negotiations into a strike.

Based on the compelling literature on the postwar "capital-labor accord," this study argues that a realistic approach to strike activity should be sensitive to two very different types of strikes: defensive, management-initiated strikes and aggressive, worker-initiated strikes.

Using an a priori categorization of a small sample of aggressive and defensive strikes, the analysis statistically divides all remaining strikes in the data sample. The statistical analysis is able to categorize accurately 84% of the strikes whose character is known a priori.

After dividing strikes, the study tests a number of hypotheses about the determinants of defensive and aggressive strike activity. Expanding on recent contributions on strike activity, the model deploys a broad vector of variables modeling the intensity of conflict and relative bargaining power between capital and labor. All along, the study anchors its hypothesis in the institutional and historical contexts in which strikes take place.

Additional statistical analysis finds substantial differences in the results for the determinants of aggressive and defensive strikes. In one case, the effects of the business cycle on the probability of the two types of strikes are opposite in sign. In a similar case, the ratio of quits to layoffs has opposite effects on defensive and aggressive strikes. These results suggest that analyses which look at all strikes together may suffer from mis-specification. In general, the results confirm two related hypotheses: 1) the probability that negotiations will fall into an aggressive strike will increase as socio-economic conditions enhance labor's strength and 2) the probability for a defensive strike will increase as conditions enhance management's strength.

Acknowledgments

This work would not have been possible without the essential contributions of two people: my dissertation advisor Davis M. Gordon and friend Stavros P. Gavroglou. I am indebted to David M. Gordon for always providing much needed guidance and patience through the years. David provided insight and help through every phase of the book. His suggestions always were constructive and supportive. For that, I am grateful. To Stavros Gavroglou, I owe a more general intellectual debt. A conceptual approach based on Marxian political economy would not frame this work were it not for our mutual and continuous intellectual explorations.

For three years, the research for this work was supported by a grant from The Center for Labor-Management Policy Studies at City University of New York. I am grateful to Victor Gotbaum, the Director, and Steve Sleigh, the Deputy Director, for their generosity and support. I could not have completed the book without the data generously provided by Cynthia Gramm. I am also grateful to the staff of the U.S. Department of Commerce, The Bureau of Labor Statistics, for providing a tape of all recorded strikes from 1952 to 1981.

I received invaluable encouragement and advice from Rhonda Williams and Bruce Pietrykowski. Both helped during the difficult beginning stages of the book. They also gave important statistical advice and suggestions on its design. Special thanks to Christy Hawkins for her encouragement and her editorial help.

Finally, I would like to thank Jeanne Schacker who emotionally supported me at every turn. Her unflagging encouragement, generosity, and friendship were invaluable for the completion of this book.

Tables

Figures

Labor Strife and the
Economy in the 1970s

CHAPTER I

Introduction

> .... strikes resulting from bargaining impasses clearly flow from the simultaneous behavior of *two* parties, not just one. It is, therefore, the behavior of both parties that any analysis must explain.
>
> Hoyt Wheeler (1982, p. 23)

1974 was a pivotal year in U.S. industrial relations. It was the year during which the U.S. experienced more strikes than any other in its history and it was the year that marked the beginnings of a dramatic decrease in strike frequency that lasted through the 1990s. Figure 1 shows the actual time-series pattern of strike activity in the U.S. for the years 1900-1995. Evidently there are three "broad cycles" of strike activity that peak roughly around World War I, World War II and the Vietnam War, respectively. Equally important are the three periods spanning the 1920s, the late 1950s-early 1960s and the late 1970s-1990s, in which strike activity fell to lower levels than the surrounding years. These long-run rhythms in strike activity reflect the unique history of the shifting systems of labor management relations in the U.S. during the twentieth century. The focus of this work lies in an attempt to relate the dramatic shift in strike activity in the 1970s to the changing structures of U.S. labor-management relations.

The explanation provided in this work for variations in strike activity in the 1970s relies heavily on an analytical framework that cites the 1970s as a period of decay in the postwar system of labor-management relations (Bowles, Gordon, Weisskopf, 1984).

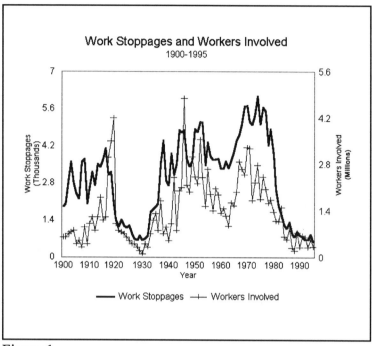

Figure 1.
Sources: Data for 1900-1905 and 1916-1981 come from the BLS, *Handbook of Labor Statistics*, (1988) Data for 1982-1995 are estimated from *Handbook of U.S. Labor Statistics*. Data for 1906-1915 are from J. I. Griffin, *Strikes: A Study in Quantitative Economics*, (1939).

According to this approach, the cooperative relationship that had been forged between capital and labor in the postwar era began to crumble in the 1970s. This cooperative relationship, known as the "capital-labor accord," was initially successful in securing a degree of peace in labor-management relations during the late 1950s and early 1960s; Figure 1 shows that strike activity fell during this period. However, strikes escalated in the late 1960s as friction developed within the framework of the accord. The accord continued to unravel in the 1970s as both labor and management struggled to stake their claim in a battle to reconstitute the system of labor-management relations. By the late 1970s, labor had lost the momentum in this struggle as management waged an offensive on workers and unions that culminated in the defeat of the Air-Traffic Controllers Association (PATCO) strike in 1981. Like the defeat of the steel strike in 1919, the PATCO defeat ushered in a decade of successful employer assaults on the union movement. Strike activity in the late 1970s and the early 1980s, like the 1920s, fell dramatically; institutionally, politically and economically, workers were too weak to strike aggressively during these periods.

The focus of this book lies in an attempt to integrate an econometric analysis of strike activity with a specific historical analysis of the complex dynamics of labor-management relations. I address two important questions: Why did strikes occur in the 1970s? What explains the annual fluctuations in these strikes?

I believe that only an approach that is sensitive to the historical specificity of working-class experience can begin to answer the perplexing theoretical problem of why strikes occur in the first place. To date, this problem has proven to be a stubborn obstacle plaguing attempts realistically to model the collective bargaining relationship. Simply stated, the theoretical problem, often called the "identification problem," points to the inherent difficulty of modeling the interdependent nature of the bargaining process when the same forces that should make one party more willing to initiate a strike, should also make the other party more willing to concede. As one party's bargaining power expands, the other party's recognition of that fact should lead to a more ready capitulation. Unemployment, for instance, may, on the one hand, be hypothesized to be negatively related to the incidence of strikes on the expectation that tighter labor markets offer workers favorable conditions for pressing their demands. On the other hand, unemployment may be positively related to the incidence of strikes on the expectation that management will press its demands and force workers to strike when workers are easier to replace from a sizeable pool of unemployed labor.

Confronted with such opposing tendencies, analysts have resorted to essentially three approaches.[1] First, many researchers have ignored the problem by modeling the behavior of only one party in the labor-management relationship. Second, others have ignored or excluded variables with opposing effects on union and employer propensity to initiate strikes. Finally, in the most compelling studies to date, investigators have explicitly acknowledged the opposing effects of many variables on union and employer decisions, but have concluded that the dynamic and interactive process of collective bargaining is theoretically indeterminant. For this reason, this last group of studies assumes that any study of strikes must rely only on empirical research to disclose the net effect of the variables under consideration. However, such attempts to eliminate the "identification problem" create complex bargaining models that specify unfalsifiable and irrefutable hypotheses.

In this presentation, I propose a theoretical model that attempts to account for the countervailing influences of many variables on union and management behavior. The second chapter summarizes and critically evaluates recent contributions to the field of industrial conflict with an eye for theories that recognize the behavior of both labor and management. The third chapter offers an alternative model of strike activity that is built on political-economic theory and situates U.S. strike activity within the historical evolution of the inherent struggle between capitalists and workers. The fourth chapter specifies the variables for an econometric model of the determinants of the capital-labor balance of power, emphasizing the importance of viewing strikes as either defensive, management initiated strikes, or aggressive, worker initiated strikes. The fifth chapter empirically divides defensive and aggressive strikes using discriminant analysis and the sixth chapter tests the hypothesized determinants of defensive and aggressive strikes with a series of probit estimations. Throughout this presentation, I argue that an adequate explanation of strike trends should focus at the micro level and should detail the opportunities and tactical resources of both parties for engaging in open conflict. When tailored to account specifically for the political-economic, institutional and historical context of industrial relations, this approach addresses the identification problem by capturing the contradictory impact of different phenomena on labor's and management's propensity to engage in open conflict.

NOTE

1. See the literature review for a full discussion of these approaches.

CHAPTER II

The Economics of Strike Activity

The literature on the economics of strikes is large and varied. Fortunately, a common thread in most recent studies is the theoretical influence of the works of J.R. Hicks and the works of Orley Ashenfelter and George E. Johnston. In this chapter, I detail the theories of Hicks and of Ashenfelter and Johnston and provide an analysis of more recent extensions of their work. I then detail two important studies that move beyond the limitations inherent in the body of work inspired by Hicks and Ashenfelter and Johnston: Michael Shalev's 1982 article, "Trade Unionism and Economic Analysis: The Case of Industrial Conflict," and Cynthia Gramm's 1984 article, "Strike Incidence and Severity: A Micro-Level Study."[1] I conclude with John Godard's 1992 study, "Strikes as Collective Voice: A Behavioral Analysis of Strike Activity."

Most economic studies of strikes explicitly attempt to respond to the so-called "Hick's Paradox." According to Hicks, in his celebrated work, *The Theory of Wages*, first published in 1932, strikes are not Pareto optimal because a strike means that the pie shrinks as the employer and the workers argue how it should be divided. Hicks highlights the difficulty in building a strike model in which both sides behave rationally—compared to a strike, any no-strike settlement represents a superior, Pareto-optimum outcome. Indeed, as John Kennan (1986, p. 1133) has pointed out: "it is impossible to build a bargaining model in which both sides behave optimally but the outcome is not Pareto optimal."

Hicks provides two suggestions that avoid the problems inherent in theorizing the existence of strikes: either the union is trying to establish the credibility of the strike threat or the existence of private information on one side of the bargaining table leads to a breakdown in negotiations. As Hicks says:

> Weapons grow rusty if unused, and a Union which never strikes may lose the ability to organize a formidable strike, so that its threats become less effective. The most able trade Union leadership will embark on strikes occasionally . . . in order to keep their weapon burnished for future use. . . . Under a system of collective bargaining, some strikes are more or less inevitable for this reason; but nevertheless the majority of strikes are doubtless the result of faulty negotiation . . . Any means which enable either side to appreciate better the position of the other will make settlement easier; adequate knowledge will always make a settlement possible (1938, pp. 146-147).

Specifically, Hicks focuses on two strike determinants: strike length and wage increases. Hicks argues that the employer's tendency to make concessions in wage bargaining is *directly* related to the expected duration of the strike while the union's resistance to making concessions is *inversely* related to its expected duration. The model is depicted in Figure 2, along lines suggested by Strauss (1983). The curve labeled EC denotes the maximum wage that employers would be prepared to pay in order to avoid strikes of given durations. At each wage on this curve, Hick's "concession curve," the expected cost of a stoppage just equals the cost of concession. The curve labeled UR denotes the minimum wages that workers would accept to avoid strikes of given durations. According to Hicks, there will be no strike if both parties are equally informed about the other's concession curve and a determinate solution will be reached at wage W* where the two curves intersect. (OZ gives the wage the employer would pay in the absence of a union.)

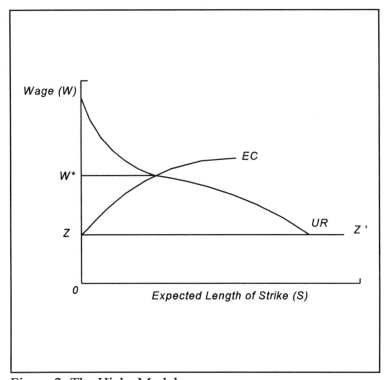

Figure 2: The Hicks Model
Source: Hirsch and Addison, (1986), p.80.

Strikes occur, according to this model, because of incomplete or asymmetric information: one party monopolizes information for itself or the other party consistently omits relevant variables from its decision calculus. The latter would arise if each side were to use different variables than the other to draw up its concession curve. In this case, one side would misjudge the opponent's rate of concession. For Hicks, such miscalculations occur accidentally or because of faulty negotiations. The primary determinant of a successfully negotiated settlement is a common understanding of the location and slopes of each other's concession curves. Unfortunately, Hicks doesn't detail the factors that influence and condition the two parties' curves. In fact, as Ashenfelter and Johnson observe:

> It is not apparent how the propensity of either or both of the parties to (a) miscalculate the intentions of the other or (b) act irrationally would be systematically related to any of the conceptually observable variables in the system (1969, p. 33).

Instead of systematically focusing on the economic conditions that influence concession rates, Hicks resorts to conjecturing about the psychology of the "working man." Hicks says, for example, that "sentimental considerations have a large influence on the willingness [of workers] to hold out for a given rate of wages" (1938, p. 153). Many theorists, most notably Hoyt Wheeler (1984), have criticized Hick's theory as a woefully inadequate conceptualization of the collective bargaining process. Hicks retains the unverified notion that anticipated strike length is the most important determinant of negotiator behavior; he focuses primarily on the union's side of the bargaining table; and he examines only strikes that result from bargaining over wages, which neglects nearly half of all U.S. strikes.[2]

Many modern treatments echo Hick's view: for example, Melvin Reder and George Neumann (1980) describe strikes as accidents and Farber (1978) views strikes as a combination of the optimizing behavior of firms and the irrational "political behavior" of workers. More recently, attempts have been made to combine rational behavior with a Hicksian formulation, leading to a large literature on asymmetrical information models.

The best of these is Martin Mauro's "Strikes as a Result of Imperfect Information" (1982). Mauro assumes that the employer disregards factors of interest to the union in forming its perception of the union's willingness to concede and that the union ignores factors important to the firm in estimating the firm's willingness to concede. Mauro assumes that the union focuses on the CPI, income taxes, real wage changes and wage changes relative to those occurring in other industries. Management, in contrast, focuses on the firm's product prices, profits and labor productivity—all items that affect the firm's derived demand for labor. Under conditions of perfect information, changes in any of these variables will not affect strike probability because each party will be aware of the changes in the other's concession curve. However, according to Mauro, under conditions of imperfect information, any changes will create a divergence in expectations because each party will form its perception of the other's concession curve by using the same variables as those used to create its own curve. In this case, strikes become a method to disclose the relevant information necessary to correct the parties' misperceptions about each other. Unfortunately, Mauro's model suffers from the same weaknesses as Hick's original formulation: it offers no compelling reasons for the systematic nature of misperceptions, nor their persistence over time. It is not clear why one party, in constructing its estimate of the opponent's concession curve, should use information different from that employed by the opponent himself. Such assumptions are not credible in the absence of a more solid theoretical and historical foundation that includes supporting evidence at the bargaining unit level of analysis.

The Ashenfelter and Johnson model (1969) departs from the Hicksian tradition by distinguishing between union officials and the rank and file. Essentially, Ashenfelter and Johnson (A-J) reject Hick's argument of "faulty negotiation" by eliminating bargaining from their model altogether. In their "political model," strikes are the mechanisms by which union leaders and the firm force the rank and file to moderate unrealistic wage demands:

> . . . The outbreak of a strike has the effect of lowering the rank and file's expectations due to the shock effect of the firm's resistance and the resultant loss of normal income. After some passage of time the leadership feels the minimum acceptable wage increase has fallen to a level at which it can safely sign with management, and the strike ends. (1969, p. 37)

For Ashenfelter and Johnson, workers are an irrational flock under the moderating influence of union officials. The leadership is assumed to assess the bargaining possibilities more accurately than the rank and file. Since they cannot risk the threats to their leadership position by signing an agreement that is less than the rank and file expects, the leadership prefers to endure a strike until workers' wage aspirations decrease to a level that the firm is prepared to pay. For its part, the firm seeks to maximize the present value of its future profit stream: it will choose the optimum tradeoff between foregone profits during the strike and increased costs after a strike subject to the union concession curve. The basic elements in the A-J model are presented in Figure 3 below. The Y_a curve represents the union concession curve facing the firm while the Y^* line indicates the minimum wage acceptable to the union after a strike of infinite length (Y_0 is the minimum acceptable wage without a strike). According to Ashenfelter and Johnson, the union concession curve can be written as:

$$Y_a = Y^* + (Y_o + Y^*)e^{-ae}$$

where ae is the rate at which Y_a decays during a strike. The P functions shown in the figure are the employer's isoprofit lines: the tradeoff between the wage offer, Y_g, and length s for any given present value of the firm. The employer would like to settle with an isoprofit curve as close to the origin as possible, since curves closer to the origin have a higher present value of the firm.

Figure 3 shows that the employer is limited to one optimum isoprofit curve because of the union concession curve. Panel (a) of figure 3 illustrates a no-strike outcome. Here, the wage increase the employer is willing to pay to avoid a strike, Y_g, is greater than or equal to the union's minimally acceptable wage increase without a strike Y_0. The firm will maximize its profits by avoiding a strike and settling with a wage increase of Y_0. In contrast, panel (b) shows the firm will maximize profits by absorbing a strike of length S_1, with a wage settlement of Y_1. This yields a profit of P_1, which is greater than the profit P_0, obtainable without a strike.

Shalev (1982) has pointed out that the main problem with this approach is that strikes are analyzed as "isolated campaigns," not a result of the bargaining process. Ashenfelter and Johnson reason that, given the political pressures on union leaders, the wage increase that is acceptable to the rank and file automatically becomes the final

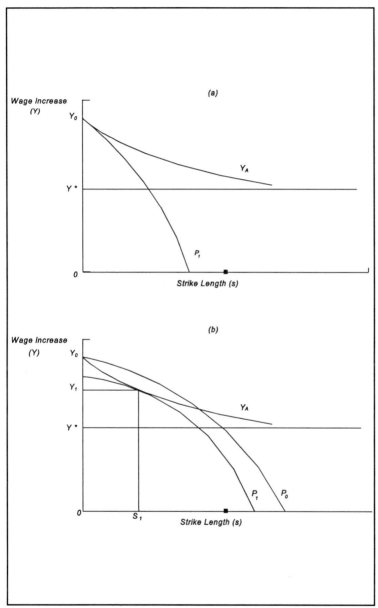

Figure 3: The Ashenfelter-Johnson Model
Source: Hirsch and Addison (1986), p.90.

bargaining position of the union and that the firm makes no concessions but simply accepts or rejects the union's demands. Ashenfelter and Johnson only model workers' exaggerated demands and elide management behavior and power. As a consequence, they ignore the interdependent behavior and strategic interaction of the collective bargaining process. In the end, they unrealistically place blame for strikes only on the union side.

For many years, Ashenfelter and Johnson's analysis was the reigning wisdom in two important ways. First, like the A-J model, most subsequent work used aggregate economic variables to explain the incidence of strikes and, second, most works accepted strike activity as procyclical (see Skeels, 1984 and Kaufman, 1982). Although their model doesn't have obvious empirical applications, Ashenfelter and Johnson suggested a specification in which the probability of a strike depends directly on the size of Y_0, the union's minimum acceptable wage. Both Y_0 and the probability of a strike are posited to be a negative function of the unemployment rate and the past rate of real wage change.

The consensus built on this approach started to break down in the 1980s. What emerged was a clear recognition that strikes result from a bargaining impasse that clearly flows from the behavior of *two* parties: workers and management. As a result, subsequent studies began to question the cyclical nature of strikes. Analyzing data from a large number of countries, Paldam and Pederson (1982) found evidence of a counter-cyclical trend in strike activity and suggested that the results are consistent with a theory that accounts for a "conflict relation" in which "a deceleration of real wages may lead to defensive strikes" (p. 518). Additionally, other theorists questioned whether macro-level measures genuinely reflect the micro-level collective bargaining they are intended to proxy. As Shalev has put it: "even though aggregate measures of strike activity have demonstrable connections to environmental forces, such measures constitute abstractions from highly diverse micro-level behaviors" (1980, p. 166).

To date, however, no analysis has adequately dealt with the behavior of both parties. As already indicated, many recent approaches have correctly considered the behavior of the two parties, but have ignored variables that have opposite effects on union and employer behavior and, consequently, have focused only on explanatory variables that influence both parties' behavior in the same direction (see Kennan, 1980 and Reder and Neumann, 1980). Two exceptions are worth describing in more detail: the works of Michael Shalev and Cynthia Gramm. Their studies recognize and try to surmount the difficulties inherent in modeling the contradictory behavior of management and workers.

Michael Shalev approaches strike activity in an overarching way, explicitly giving theoretical priority to power resources over expectations or highly abstract inferences about the parties' perceptions of their economic well-being: " . . . the desire to inflict costs on an opponent is of little practical importance absent the ability to do so" (1980, p. 155). He theorizes that economic, political and organizational factors are power resources influencing workers' and management's propensity to strike. He operationalizes his theoretical model by developing *a priori* hypotheses about the effects of specific aggregate forces on the ability of management and labor to engage in open conflict. Unfortunately, many variables operationalized in his model don't faithfully reflect the theory on which they are based because he develops arbitrary specifications in dealing with the identification problem. He argues, for instance, that "net of their organizational strength, scarcity is the primary determinant of workers' bargaining power in a market economy, whereas the power resources of employers can be assumed to 'fluctuate much more sluggishly than those of labor.' Hence the unemployment rate is likely to affect workers' calculations, and a net negative influence is predicted"[3] (1980, p. 157). Although he admits that unemployment is also a determinant of management's bargaining power ("strikers are easier to replace when there is a large pool of unemployed" 1980, p. 159), he doesn't persuasively explain why management is more "sluggish" than labor in it response to changes in unemployment. Certainly his quote from Snyder is inadequate, especially since Snyder, contrary to Shalev's express purposes, uses it as a justification for ignoring employers' resources and power altogether.

Shalev makes similar *ad hoc* assumptions about the differential responses of management and labor to other variables that affect their bargaining power and willingness to initiate strikes. Notwithstanding his comprehensive theoretical approach, his empirical model is misspecified because he doesn't adequately operationalize the institutional resources and power of capital and labor. He doesn't operationalize management's ability to threaten workers with capital flight nor management's inherent leverage embodied in parallel production. Likewise, he doesn't fully model labor's capacity for collective action, ignoring variables such as the rate of unionization. In other words, he doesn't operationalize what he theoretically considers the struggle "over management rights" (1980, p. 159). Shalev recognizes some of these problems and admits that a superior method would base a model of conflict at a disaggregated level. Specifically, he points to the difficulty of testing certain micro-level hypotheses at the macro-level when many variables at the macro-level are stable, masking differences and instabilities across different sectors and industries. For this reason, he explicitly eschews empirically specifying certain power resources, like the unionization rate:

> [The theory] seemingly justifies the inclusion of the rate of unionization in the model, but over the period considered, aggregate union density has varied so little that this did not seem necessary. However, in individual sectors of the economy, it is of course highly likely that a positive association could be detected. (1980, p. 155)

As Shalev later points out, it is, however, important to test his entire theoretical framework at a disaggregated level of analysis. Fortunately, Cynthia Gramm addresses this problem by modeling the collective bargaining relationship at a bargaining unit of analysis, using a comprehensive micro-level data set.

Like Shalev, Cynthia Gramm (1986) takes the important methodological step of considering the behavior of both parties involved in the collective bargaining relationship. According to Gramm, the employer chooses the strategy that minimizes its expected loss of profit, while the union chooses the action that maximizes its net expected gains. If a gap between the employer's offer and the union's demand remains at the strike deadline, each party faces a choice: concession, in which case a strike is averted, or holding out, in which case a strike may be precipitated. According to Gramm, the probability that the employer will risk a strike (or its continuation) by not conceding is:

(1) $P(\text{Risk Strike}_e) = 1$ if $E(\text{Loss}^s) < E(\text{Loss}^{ns})$, 0 otherwise,

where $E(\text{Loss})$ is the expected loss of profits and the superscripts s and ns refer to strike and no strike respectively.

Similarly, the probability that a union will risk a strike is:

(2) $P(\text{Risk Strike}_u) = 1$ if $E(\text{Net Gain}^s) > E(\text{Net Gain}^{ns})$, 0 otherwise

where $E(\text{Net Gain})$ is the union's expected gain from the settlement.

For Gramm, many factors contribute to an employer's estimate of its expected losses due to a strike—the marginal profit loss (MPLS) associated with each day of interrupted production, the employer's ability to retain market share (MS), and its ability to remain solvent during a strike (FS). The magnitude of these losses increases with strike duration. Gramm recognizes that an employer's estimate of its losses during a strike is dependent on its subjective estimate of the union's concession rate, $E(C^U)$. She formalizes employers' behavior in the following manner:

(3) $P(\text{Risk Strike} = 1) = f[\text{MPL, MS, FS}, E(C^U)]$

where $f_1 < 0$, and $f_2, f_3, f_4, > 0$.

On the union side, Gramm hypothesizes that a union's expected net gain during a strike is higher, the lower the cost of striking. For Gramm, the main cost to the union consists of the marginal wage loss per worker for each additional day that the strike continues (Wage). Additional costs include workers' demand for current income and the threat of permanent job loss to replacements (JL). These costs are moderated if the strikers can find a substitute income source (SI). Gramm, recognizing that these costs mount as a strike continues, postulates that the union's expected length of a strike depends upon its subjective estimate of the employer's concession rate $E(C^E)$. Finally, Gramm postulates that workers' expectations (EXPECT) play a role in a union's willingness to strike. Sounding like Ashenfelter and

Johnston, she says: "when the rank and file's expectations exceed what the employer is willing or able to offer, union leaders may be unable to persuade them that their demands are unrealistic" (1986, p. 363). In summary, for unions:

(4) $P(\text{Risk Strike} = 1) = g[\text{WAGE, } E(C^E), \text{DI, JL, SI, EXPECT}]$

where g_1, g_3, g_4, < 0, and g_2, g_5, $g_6 > 0$.

By theorizing that the collective bargaining process includes the dynamic behavior of both parties, Cynthia Gramm faces the identification problem when she tries to estimate structural choice equations (3) and (4). Neither $E(C^E)$ nor $E(C^U)$ is observable. The employer must estimate C^U from the available information on factors that influence union willingness to strike, just as the union must estimate C^E from the available information on factors influencing the employer's willingness to take a strike. When the appropriate substitutions are made for $E(C^E)$ and $E(C^U)$ in equations (3) and (4) respectively, the right hand-sides of the two equations are identical. They are unidentified (Pindyck and Rubinfeld, 1981, p. 324).

Gramm (1986) resolves this problem by estimating a reduced form model that estimates the probability of a strike's occurrence at the bargaining level unit of analysis:

(5) $P(\text{Strike} = 1) = f(\text{Wage, DI, JL, JL, SI, EXPECT, MPL, MS, FS})$

According to Gramm, each estimated coefficient represents the net effect of the countervailing effects of the associated explanatory variable on the union's willingness to strike and the employer's willingness to take a strike.

Clearly, Gramm addresses the identity problem by eschewing a theory of strike activity. Instead, she lets the empirical data in her model reveal the links between strikes and economic conditions and on this basis assesses the relative importance of each variable on the union's and employer's propensity to strike: " . . . the advantage is that the model, by explicitly acknowledging that most explanatory variables have opposing effects on union and employer decisions, depicts the bargaining process more realistically" (1986, p.365). While making an important step towards a more realistic and robust specification, this model, by design, doesn't relate its findings to a formal theory that can explain the underlying socio-economic processes which condition the relationship between strike activity and the behavior of management and workers. Important as it may be to realize that growth in product demand has a significant, negative effect on strike incidence during the period of her study, a more penetrating analysis would provide convincing reasons as to why such a result is endemic to the behavior of management and labor at that particular stage of capitalist development.

Throughout her presentation, Gramm (1986) claims that her approach improves on previous studies by assuming that the bargaining parties are "rational"—that they are able to learn and that they do not consistently lack or disregard information concerning one or more factors that influence the opponent's concession rate. However, if this were the case, it is not clear why strikes occur in the first place. In fact, her approach still requires the assumption of either myopic or "irrational" behavior on the part of one of the parties or of incomplete information: if each party were informed of the other party's concession rate, strikes should not occur because any no-strike settlement would represent a superior, Pareto-optimum outcome compared to a strike. In other words, Hicks' "paradox" still haunts her model.

Any solution to the Hicks paradox must integrate the lived experience of the participants involved. The unfolding historical evolution and institutionalization of the balance of power between labor and management governs both parties' assessment of the possible and informs their sense of what is fair and unfair. An analysis of strike activity cannot be abstracted from the particular time or place that condition the willingness and ability of labor and management to engage in industrial warfare. A specific decision to strike may seem irrational in terms of the total resources foregone; financially, both parties could have been better off if there had not been a strike. However, when coupled with the understanding that an implicit social contract has been broken by one of the parties, an economic analysis can conclude that a strike is historically and politically rational. In general, one party may be willing to risk financial loss in an effort to preserve accustomed prerogatives, like seniority; in another case, one party may be willing to risk a short run non-Pareto outcome in an ongoing effort to establish new long-run prerogatives, like union recognition. Failure to relate strike theory in a determinant way to the historical systems and institutions governing the dynamics of labor-management relations is likely to lead to arbitrary assumptions.

Indeed, Gramm's theoretical justification for several of her hypotheses about strike activity seem rather arbitrary. For instance, why should WAGE (the absolute value of workers' wages) be negatively related to the probability that a union will risk a strike? For Gramm, as already indicated, workers will be more reluctant to strike when they have more to risk during a strike. As an alternative, Shalev has suggested that the probability that a union will risk a strike depends more directly on the relative wages of other union members: "for political reasons both internal and external to unions, pay relativities are critical to workers' conceptions of wage equity" (1980, p. 158). Wheeler (1984) has argued that the relationship between strike activity and variables like real wages and unemployment is reasonably explicable on a number of contradictory grounds. High real wages might exist precisely because a union is strong, able and willing to strike. Contrary to Gramm's expectations, high real wages may be positively related to a union's ability to risk a strike on the assumption that high real wages reflect a strong, cohesive union. Wheeler has also suggested that the absolute level of real wages may or may not have an influence on strike activity, depending upon the issues involved in the strike. All of these contending theoretical arguments make assumptions about the behavior of labor and management that cannot be adjudicated without reference to the historical patterns and understandings embedded in the system governing labor-management relations at the time.[4]

This leads to a final problem with Gramm's analysis. Empirical tests are usually conducted with the express purpose of either supporting or rejecting a given theory. Theory informs the choice of data and indicators. However, the nature of Gramm's approach is so broad that there is little justification for either limiting the analysis to the variables included, indicating underspecification bias, or including many of the variables in the study, indicating overspecification bias.

More recently, John Godard (1992) has correctly censured the strike literature for not adequately accounting for the broader institutional context of labor-management relations. He proposes a more definitive, institutional approach to understanding the behavioral determinants of strike activity. This approach is built on three central arguments: (1) the decision to strike is made by workers and their agents; (2) all strikes require a mobilization of workers that is predicated on workers' notions of fairness and legitimacy; and (3) strikes are a natural tendency of capitalist societies because workers are institutionally subordinate to management authority. Coined the "collective voice approach," this theory views strikes as the primary means by which workers express their collective discontent.

Certainly, Godard makes an important contribution to the strike literature by situating strikes within the inherent institutional conflict between labor and management. He focuses on workers' notions of fairness and equity and, importantly, he proposes to look at management's behavior by positing that "hard bargaining" may be a source of worker discontent that can lead to strikes. Unfortunately, like Shalev, Godard resorts to ad hoc specifications of his behavioral variables.

Godard's approach is not systematically informed by a theory that places institutional conflict within an historical account of the changes in the balance of power between labor and management. Without such a detailed, historical approach, he is forced to alternate between opposing abstract explanations for strike activity. For instance, he admits that favorable market conditions have opposing effects on labor and management, but concludes that "where management's willingness to accommodate or "buy off" workers demands is high, the initial militancy of worker's can be expected to dissipate, as workers have less reason to incur the costs of a strike. . . . Favorable market conditions should be associated with lower strike activity" (1992, p. 169). However, later, when faced with unexpected results, he posits that workers expect management to be able to grant concessions and are also less fearful of their jobs during growing markets. Therefore, the perceived effectiveness of strikes during favorable market conditions should lead to more strikes. Indeed, both explanations are logical, but his theory is rendered arbitrary in its attempts to accommodate both of them.

A more compelling model of strike activity should combine the strengths of Shalev's, Gramm's and Godard's approaches. Such a model should: (a) move beyond earlier literature by looking at the behavior of both parties and accounting for the opposing effects of some variables on the union's and employer's propensity to strike; (b) assume at least the possibility of the rationality of both classes; (c) provide a determinant theory that offers a convincing specification of expected relationships; (d) overcome weaknesses of aggregate specifications by utilizing Gramm's micro-level data; and (e) incorporate socio-economic, technical and organizational factors as power resources influencing workers' and management's propensity to strike.

NOTES

1. For a comprehensive survey of the literature on the economics of strikes, see Kennan (1986).

2. I review the breakdown of strike activity below in Chapter V.

3. The interior quote is taken from Snyder (1977, p.330).

4. For an interesting discussion on the compatible relationship between econometric models and historical materialism, see Kalecki (1975).

CHAPTER III

Postwar Industrial Relations in The U.S.

In this chapter, the historical context of postwar strike activity is briefly presented. It is suggested here that the eruption of strikes in the 1970s has it roots in the historical fluctuations and rhythms of postwar industrial relations. As will be argued later, a theory of strike activity and subsequent empirical work should be particularly sensitive to the evolving struggle between labor and capital. As Shalev points out, quoting Commons: " . . . the socialists call it class struggle. It is a continuous bargain every day and hour" (1919, p. 24). The axis of this struggle is the "power" of the two contending classes—what, as Shalev points out, is the "fighting frontier of control" or the problem of managerial rights.

As in authoritarian states, workers cannot elect or appoint their rulers within the employment relation and they have little or no legal right to participate in the governance of the organization for which they work. Turmoil is likely as workers try to affect the conditions of their employment from a position of inherent, institutional weakness. The unrest between the two sides is constant and durable, a continuous struggle for influence and advantage; strikes occur when a complex of forces at given point in time affects the strength and interest of workers or employers enough for one party to initiate overt conflict.

Strikes then serve as one of the primary means by which workers collectively express their discontent.

In an important sociological study of strikes, Hiller (1928) began to dissect the forces behind the timing of strike activity, emphasizing the notion of "tactical advantage." Hiller argued that in times of an "active market" unions are prone to launch aggressive strikes because of employer economic vulnerability (due to scarcity of strike breakers) and the relatively strong financial position of workers and unions. In periods of economic decline, the employer becomes relatively impervious to union pressures while the union becomes economically more vulnerable. In such situations, for Hiller (1928, p. 128), the majority of strikes are "defensive conflicts to preserve the existing terms." For Hiller, any examination of strike activity should separately analyze the conditions surrounding two types of strikes: defensive and aggressive.

Building on this approach, I propose that a model of the timing of these disparate strikes should be built on the analytical framework proposed by Gordon, Edwards and Reich (1982). This framework is sensitive to historical detail and relatively comprehensive in its inclusion of political, social and economic factors. Such a broad historical perspective is a useful point of departure for defining defensive and aggressive strikes and for examining strike activity in the 1970s in a determinant way.

According to Gordon, Edwards and Reich (1982), capitalism experiences historically specific stages called social structures of accumulation (SSA). Each SSA has its own particular institutional arrangement that organizes capitalist accumulation for an extended period of time. Typically, these stages last for several decades: they embody a certain set of laws, institutions and class relations that establish customary ways of producing and consuming, structure the organization of the government, and shape peoples' vision of themselves and those around them. Each SSA goes through a common life-cycle: exploration, consolidation and decay:

> We propose that each stage shaping the labor process and labor market structure has a lifetime whose adolescence begins in the previous period of economic crisis, whose maturity begins with the

construction of a new social structure of accumulation, and whose decline spreads as economic crisis deepens once again. (Gordon, Reich and Edwards, 1982, p. 10).

The SSA analysis suggests that forces endogenous to each SSA engender an economic crisis that requires institutional restructuring in order to renew capitalist stability and growth. During this crisis, spreading stagnation and escalating tensions between labor and management undermine institutions that had dominated in the previous SSA. This period is referred to as the period of decay. As the crisis continues and intensifies, capitalists experiment with new methods of labor management in order to restore a favorable climate for capitalist accumulation. This phase is called the period of exploration. The most promising resolutions, shaped by the impact of workers collective struggle, are incorporated into a new social structure of accumulation. Gordon, Edwards and Reich refer to this phase as the period of consolidation. The emergence of a new SSA critically depends upon the nature of capitalists' and workers' collective struggle:

> Although there is no guarantee that a successful new social structure
> of accumulation will emerge, if one does it will reflect the alignment
> of class forces . . . that produce it. Thus, the rise of a new social
> structure of accumulation depends upon the previous downswing and
> more specifically on the concrete historical conditions that the period
> of downswing bequeaths to the major classes (1982, p. 31).

Once consolidation proceeds and production conditions stabilize, the struggle between labor and management should abate.

Any historical study of the U.S. must recognize the thirties as an important juncture in industrial relations: a new social structure of accumulation began to take shape as the country emerged from a depression and as class conflict intensified. The decay of the previous social structure of accumulation led to the Great Depression of the mid 1930s and initiated a period of struggle over the terms of a new institutionalization of labor-management relations.[1]

In the years prior to 1934-35, unions existed in a predominantly non-institutionalized setting (Snyder, 1975). Union recognition, collective bargaining and labor-management contractual agreements were not uniformly codified: labor law was primarily developed by state courts applying common law concepts with little statutory guidance (Getman, 1988). In addition, before 1935 there was no direct legal precedent dealing with strikes. In all too many cases, striking workers would be imprisoned and their unions would be served with injunctions and destroyed (Goldfield, 1989). In the early 1930s labor radicalism and militancy, catapulted into national prominence by the 1934 strike wave, paved the way for a steady stream of legislation that wiped out the legal basis for many antiunion employer tactics. The most significant piece of legislation was the National Labor Relations Act (the Wagner Act), enacted in 1935.

Section 7 is at the heart of the NLRA. It grants to employees "the rights to self-organization to join or assist labor organizations to bargain collectively through representatives of their own choosing and to engage in concerted activities for the purpose of collective bargaining and other mutual aid or protection." [2] One of the key aspects of the new law was the formation of the National Labor Relations Board, a panel that was assigned the task of administrating the NLRA and resolving all conflicting claims in almost all labor disputes. Among other things, the Board decides when a union representation election is to be held, the eligible voters, and the results.

The Wagner Act envisioned collective bargaining as the outcome of labor-management relations—a process by which employee participation and industrial peace could be achieved, management rights ensured, and rival claims articulated and adjudicated through grievance procedures (Gould, 1986). Workers' struggles throughout the country in 1934-35 framed the terms of the debate over passage of the Act. According to its supporters, the primacy of industrial peace depended upon the Act's passage. On June 18, 1935, the last day of floor debate in the House, Representative Withrow of Wisconsin argued " . . . strikes have been prevalent in this country during the last two years . . . the passage of this legislation is the only cure for the labor difficulties which have been characteristic for the past few years" (NLRB, 1985, p. 3132). In a similar fashion, Representative Sweeny of Ohio said on the same date that "unless this Wagner-Connery dispute bill is passed we are going to have an epidemic of strikes that has never been witnessed before in this country" (NLRB, 1985, p. 1368). Clearly, many felt that strikes could be averted and industrial peace realized only if strikes were legally recognized. As the Act itself proclaims:

> Experience has further demonstrated that certain practices by some labor organizations, their officers and members have the intent or the necessary effect of burdening commerce by preventing the free flow of goods in such commerce through strikes and other forms of industrial unrest or through concerted activities which impair the interest of the public in the free flow of such commerce. The elimination of such practices is a necessary condition to the assurance of the rights herein guaranteed . . . nothing in this act shall be construed so as either to interfere with or impede or diminish in any way the right to strike (NLRA, section 7).

The period immediately following the passage of the Wagner Act was the point in time during which strikes were given their greatest legal protection. For the only time in American history, there was not only a legal right to engage in primary strikes over wages and working conditions, but strikes for purposes of organizing, obtaining recognition, claiming work, or aiding other unions were also protected against either employer or judicial action (Getman, 1988).

However, the struggle to reconstitute the new social structure of accumulation didn't end with the passage of the Wagner Act. Many important disputes over strike activity were left untouched in 1935. Were a sit-down or other partial strikes protected? Could an employer continue operations during a strike by assigning supervisors to do the job? Could he hire replacements? If so, could he assure these replacements the opportunity for continued employment after the strike was over? In addition, during the late 1940s, capital launched a concerted effort to scale back many of labor's gains embodied in the Wagner Act. This was coupled with an anti-communist purge of the CIO between 1946 and 1950 (Caute, 1978).

Capital's counteroffensive culminated in 1947 with the passage of the Taft-Hartley Act. This legislation, drafted by the National Association of Manufacturers, dramatically curtailed unions' right to strike (Gordon, Edwards, Reich, 1982). Section 8(b)(4) of the Taft

Hartley outlawed secondary strikes, rejecting the idea that it was legitimate for employees of different employers to make common cause with each other—a concept previously embedded in the language of the Wagner Act. The Taft-Hartley Act also resurrected the possibility of court injunctions against unions that violated the secondary strike provision. In addition, section 8 of the Act forbade certain types of recognitional and jurisdictional strikes.

By the early 1950s, a host of strike issues were settled in management's favor. Sit-down strikes were not protected by the law; management had the right to maintain production using supervisors; striking workers could be permanently replaced; and honoring a picket line could lead to discharge. In addition, strikes were rendered illegal if they occurred during the term of the collective agreement and if they were about an issue that did not come within the statutory phrase "rates of pay, wages, hours of employment, or other conditions of employment" (Getman, 1988, p. 12).

These legislative resolutions set boundaries for the new, emerging system of labor-management relations. This new system involved much more than just government statutes. During the 1950s, labor-management behavior and practices became more and more routinized and regularized as acceptable behavior became defined in terms of a common, unwritten accord. This accord involved a *quid pro quo* between labor and management that incorporated the main purposes of the NLRA: the maintenance of an orderly and profitable economy by ensuring industrial peace (Flaherty, 1986; Naples, 1986; and Gordon Edwards and Reich, 1982). In this context, strikes, though legal, were viewed as an unacceptable and disruptive outcome of labor-management relations.

For its part, what Bowles, Gordon and Weisskopf (1984) call the "capital-labor accord" was premised on workers relinquishing all claims over production, investment and international economic policy in return for a higher degree of job security and a stable gain on real earnings. Through the late 1950s and early 1960s, this institutional structure contributed to industrial stability; all signs seemed to point to continued growth, the end of industrial conflict, the end of economic insecurity and even, as Daniel Bell (1960) put it, "the end of ideology." The spendable hourly earnings of production workers rose at an annual average of 2.1 percent from 1948 to 1966 while unemployment fell to a postwar low of 3.85 percent in 1966 (Bowles, Gordon and Weisskopf, 1984, p. 24). Working conditions similarly improved—the industrial accident rate fell by 30 percent between 1948 and the early 1960s and the number of workers involved in strikes fell dramatically (Naples, 1986, p. 119). Indeed, industrial conflict and worker resistance fell in this period to an all time low as both labor and capital received real material benefits; the new social structure of accumulation initially was successful in maintaining economic order and industrial peace.

Despite the early success of the accord in containing and redirecting class conflict, the accord began to unravel in the late 1960s. The very institutional stability that fostered the postwar boom provided the economic context within which workers escalated their struggle against capital. Recent literature has identified several related but distinct empirical components of the decay of the postwar capital-labor accord (Bowles, Gordon, Weisskopf, 1984; Naples, 1988).[3]

First, rapid accumulation and sustained low employment in the 1960s decreased workers' economic vulnerability and, hence, expanded their bargaining power. With secular declines in unemployment, workers were better able to pay off debts, accumulate resources and increase strike funds. Furthermore, Johnson's Great Society, the welfare component of the institutional arrangement, further reduced the impact of unemployment on workers' well-being. As a result, there were more quits, absenteeism and strikes, including wildcat strikes and strikes over working conditions (Naples, 1987). Naples (1986) argues that this unraveling of the truce initiated a decline in productivity growth.

Capital responded to the ensuing profit squeeze by intensifying supervision in an effort to increase the intensity and productivity of labor. This led to a dramatic increase in the injury frequency rate in manufacturing and a further erosion of the legitimacy of capitalist control of the workplace (Arno, 1982). Workers' resistance spread: the percent of tentative contract settlements rejected by rank and file jumped from 8.7 percent in 1963-1964 to 14.2 percent in 1966-1967 and the terrain of the capital labor conflict shifted, as aggressive strikes over working conditions further escalated (Naples, 1987).

Capital control of the labor process was disrupted and, as a consequence, the postwar social structure of accumulation entered a crisis. By the mid 1970s, the economic crisis and resulting class struggle developed into a stalemate as the two contending classes jockeyed for position in the struggle over institutional restructuring. Through the stalemate, corporations resorted to their ultimate weapons: capital flight and capital strike. From 1973 to 1979 investment growth rates declined and the economy stagnated as corporations refused to invest in the soured economic environment (Bowles and Edwards, 1985). While domestic investment growth fell in the mid 1970s, net foreign direct investment abroad, after a slowdown in the 68-73 period, increased. Capital strike and flight became a mechanism for capital to discipline labor and regain its commanding economic power. Higher unemployment and the increased globalization of capital left workers and communities more vulnerable to corporate demands. As Bluestone and Harrison, referring to capital flight, note in their book, *The Deindustrialization of America*, (1982, p. 128):

> It is apparent that by the 1970s, U.S. corporate managers had found a way to respond to the crisis of competition, costs and profits by reorganizing production on an explicitly interregional, international scale. Capital mobility itself, whether enacted or merely threatened, was becoming a mechanism for altering the very foundations of labor-management relations.

After 1974, these management offenses and the higher unemployment rate had a chilling effect on aggregate strike activity, which dropped markedly along with the rate of unionization (see figure 1). Also, during this period, the *type* of workers' protest shifted. As expected, aggression by management motivated workers to defend themselves collectively. Workers decreased their individual actions, lowering the quit rate substantially and escalated their collective defense, increasing the number of strikes over job security (Naples, 1987).

The analysis which follows in subsequent chapters studies the last years of labor's ascendancy and the following years of the capital-labor stalemate, 1971-1980. During this period, the postwar accord between labor and capital set the boundaries for legitimate forms and objectives of industrial conflict. The accord included industry-wide and pattern-bargaining, union recognition, long term contracts, automatic wage adjustments through cost of living allowances (COLAs) and productivity increases, mutually accepted work rules and the redirection of industrial conflict away from strikes towards grievance procedures and arbitration.

This system of control included jobs that were finely divided and frequently situated within job ladders and internal promotional systems (Gordon, Edwards, Reich, 1982). Hiring, firing and promotions up the ladder of internally divided jobs depended upon established rules and procedures that were systematically laid out and regularized. From the workers' perspective, the critical gains were job security within an array of finely divided jobs and the growth of real wages, whereas from capital's perspective, owners gained the relative freedom of enterprise and the ability to maintain productivity growth. As Gordon, Edwards and Reich (1982) emphasize, this compromise between labor and management tended to focus collective bargaining on wages and fringe benefits, leaving the determination of working conditions to management's engineers and labor relations experts.

Within this institutional framework, strikes occurred when the economic and political foundations of the "mature collective bargaining" process were violated either by management or by workers. It is assumed in the following analysis, then, that non-wage defensive strikes were a response to threats on unions' accustomed prerogatives and included strikes over job loss, seniority, the division of work and management efforts to break the union. Aggressive strikes over non-wage issues threatened management's freedom of enterprise and disrupted management's administration of the plant's operations. Included in such cases were strikes over plant administration and working conditions.

This approach addresses the identification problem in two related ways. First, I identify defensive and aggressive strikes according to the issues of contention during shifts in the balance of power between the two classes. This disaggregation, once accomplished, allows one set of strikes to respond differently to behavioral and power characteristics than the other set, avoiding the theoretical conundrum of aggregate studies. In other words, the different responses of labor and capital to changing conditions are built directly into the model. For example, the number of strikes wherein labor defensively responds to capital aggressions is allowed to rise as unemployment rises during slack market conditions, while the number of strikes when management is vulnerable to labor's demands is allowed to rise as unemployment falls during tight market conditions.

Second, as already indicated, the stability of the capital-labor accord was undermined in the 1970's when both classes, at different times, escalated conflict outside the accord in response to increases in power. Strikes occurred as one class initiated conflicts over issues outside the accord, while the other class, protecting its prerogatives within the accord and lacking relative power, refused to capitulate. Strikes over all issues increased in the early 1970s as the postwar capital-labor accord deteriorated and both capital and labor struggled to reconstitute the terms of labor-management relations. Aggressive strikes escalated as labor's strength increased relative to capital's, *despite* capital's recognition of labor's increasing strength; and defensive strikes escalated when capital's power increased, *despite* labor's recognition of that fact.

In summary, the "identification problem" involving the simultaneous, countervailing behavior of the classes is approached in this analysis with a historically specific study that places the existence of strikes in a model which captures the contradictory impact of different phenomena on labor's and capital's propensity to engage in strikes. As conditions improved for labor in the 1970s, I assume that labor aggressively attempted to establish new, unestablished prerogatives by demanding greater control over plant administration and working conditions. In such cases, management refused and aggressive strikes occurred. In contrast, as conditions improved for management, I assume that it attacked labor's established job security and work rules. Labor refused to capitulate and defensive strikes occurred.

NOTES

1. Unless otherwise noted, I have relied heavily in this historical discussion on the following sources: Bowles, Gordon and Weisskopf, 1984; Goldfield, 1989; Gordon, Edwards and Reich, 1982; Naples, 1986.

2. National Labor Act of 1935, ch. 372,49, codified as amended at 29 U.S.C. 151-169. For a full discussion on National Labor Relations Act, see Getman, 1988.

3. According to Bowles, Gordon and Weisskopf (1984), it is important to recognize that the decay of the postwar social structure of accumulation in the U.S. occurred along four dimensions: the breakdown of the capital-labor accord, the decline of U.S. international domination, the erosion of the legitimacy of capitalism embedded in the postwar capitalist-citizen accord and the increase of international capitalist competition.

CHAPTER IV

A Structuralist Model of Strikes in U.S. Manufacturing in the 1970s

A. Objectives.

In general, I propose to analyze strike activity for two major purposes:

A. To test the empirical possibility of dividing intercontractual strike activity into two qualitatively unique dimensions of industrial conflict: *defensive* and *aggressive* working class militancy.

B. To test a structural model of the determinants of defensive and aggressive strike propensity, considering the importance of union structure, industrial characteristics, discrimination, capitalist power and economic control variables as determinants of these two forms of strike activity.

In the following sections, I will elaborate on the methodologies used to pursue these two tasks and specify the variables that both methodologies employ in a quantitative study of strike activity in U.S. manufacturing from 1971 through 1980.

B. Methodologies

1. Defensive and Aggressive Strikes.

Numerous theorists have persuasively shown the importance of disaggregating strike activity (Wheeler, 1984; Shorter and Tilly, 1978; Naples, 1981).

Michele Naples (1981) provides the most compelling evidence to date that defensive strikes behave differently over time than aggressive strikes. She conducts a factor analysis on a number of indicators of strike activity and finds three qualitatively different principal components of working class militancy: OUTRUCE, DEFENSIVE, and TRADITIONAL. OUTRUCE is highly correlated with the number of strikes and the proportion of strikes over working conditions. For Naples, this measure captures workers' aggressive militancy that goes outside the bonds of the postwar accord. DEFENSIVE represents defensive actions by workers in the face of company aggression and is positively correlated with the percent of workers and of workdays lost to strikes over job-security, and negatively related to OUTRUCE. TRADITIONAL loads heavily on the number of strikers as a proportion of the labor force and the proportion of working time lost to strikes. Naples acknowledges that more empirical work is required before a measure of traditional militancy within the truce can be developed. At the very least, the results of her analysis provide preliminary evidence for the contrasting behavior of aggressive (OUTRUCE) and defensive (DEFENSIVE) strikes and suggests that these different dimensions of labor militancy should be treated differently.

With defensive strikes, workers are better able to maintain their past gains and practices, and, with aggressive strikes, they are better able to achieve new ones. Thus, at the first level of approximation, I will view defensive strikes as management-initiated and aggressive strikes as worker-initiated. However, numerous problems must be addressed as the analysis becomes more focused.

It is not always altogether clear when striking workers are acting defensively or seeking better arrangements. This is especially true when analyzing wage strikes. While some strikes are clearly initiated to prevent wage cuts, similar defensive strikes are conducted to maintain real wage gain patterns. Clearly, a theoretically justified benchmark is required to be able to classify such strikes.

I have argued above that the postwar accord between labor and capital sets the boundaries for legitimate forms and objectives of industrial conflict. Defensive and aggressive non-wage strikes are defined by the implicit terms of this accord. I include as aggressive, those strikes that are over physical shop conditions and strikes over insubordination, discharge and disciplinary suspension. I define defensive strikes as those that are over seniority, layoffs and the division of work (see chapter V for a detailed delineation of aggressive and defensive non-wage strike issues). Unfortunately, this approach still leaves the division of wage strikes unresolved. Further, the strike literature provides little guidance in solving this difficulty; even Naples' approach leaves the issue of wage strikes and their place within the capital-labor accord unexplored.

Nevertheless, it is reasonable to assume that the variety of economic and institutional conditions that govern the breakdown of non-wage strikes mirror the conditions necessary for the division of wage strikes. Any serious violation of the capital labor bargaining accord depends upon economic and institutional circumstances that condition shifts in bargaining power. I assume that these circumstances are similar for wage and non-wage strikes. The capital-labor accord set the terms for the social truce between labor and management and set the boundaries for legitimate forms of industrial conflict. Strikes result from labor or management attempting to use its relative power to change the terms of the accord, whether wage or non-wage. According to this argument, the defending party refuses to capitulate because its conceptions of legitimacy and fairness are violated by an attack on the established, if implicit, accord.

This approach provides the basis for using a statistical technique called discriminant analysis. Using discriminant analysis, I distinguish between defensive and aggressive wage strikes on the basis of a number of hypothesized bargaining power variables (to be specified below). The value of the coefficients on these variables is determined by non-wage strikes and then used to assign wage strikes as defensive or aggressive. This approach, therefore, assumes that these coefficients are the same across wage and non-wage strikes.

2. Strike Propensity.

I argued earlier that two problems plague the most recent empirical literature on strike activity. First, much of it suffers from aggregation bias and, second, researchers have had to rely on imperfect proxies of the propensity to strike. The first weakness is addressed in this study by categorizing strikes as either aggressive or defensive. Cynthia Gramm (1986) has resourcefully surmounted the second problem. She measures the propensity to strike as the proportion of negotiations involving a strike and conducts her analysis at the micro-level, using the negotiation of a collective bargaining agreement as her unit of observation.

Gramm's measure makes significant advances over previous studies for many reasons. The most commonly used measure of strike "propensity" has been strike frequency (the number of strikes occurring during a given period of time for the economy, industry or union; see Paldam and Pederson, 1982; Edwards, 1977; Snyder, 1977). Gramm highlights two significant problems with this measure (Gramm, 1987, p. 1). First, the frequency measure includes strikes occurring outside the context of contract negotiations. Flaherty has shown that the determinants of contract negotiation strikes differ from those of wildcat strikes (Flaherty, 1983). Failure to exclude these types of strikes runs the risk of measurement error and can lead to flawed conclusions. Second, the frequency with which an event occurs doesn't reflect the probability of its occurrence. The magnitude of the strike frequency measure depends upon the opportunities to strike—upon the frequency of negotiations. Without controlling for the opportunity to strike, the relationship between strike frequency and other variables found in many strike studies may actually be capturing the relationship between negotiation frequency and those variables.

Some analysts have included a probabilistic measure of strike activity by including proxies for opportunities to strike on the right side of their equations. Ashenfelter and Johnston, arguing that the number of contract negotiations doesn't vary form year to year, assert that they only need to control for seasonal variation by adding quarterly dummies as independent variables (Ashenfelter and Johnston, 1969). This approach is dubious for two reasons: 1) a cursory glance of the annual issues of the Wage Calendar and Bargaining Calendar (U.S. Bureau of Labor Statistics, 1970-1980) reveals a large variation in the annual number of negotiations; 2) it well established that strike activity has always fluctuated seasonally, even before the development of formal bargaining contracts (Edwards, 1977; Griffin, 1939). For this reason, seasonal dummies cannot be taken solely as proxies for contract expirations.

Other studies that try to control for contract negotiations confront additional problems with data availability. Kaufman (1981) includes the natural log of the number of major contract expirations on the right hand side of a model of the natural log of the number of strikes. Like earlier models, this approach inappropriately aggregates strikes that occur during the term of an agreement with those that occur during renegotiations. Unfortunately, this study is additionally problematic because the strike frequency series is constructed by aggregating across all bargaining units while the contract expiration series is obtained by aggregating across only those relationships that involve 1000 workers or more. Unfortunately, evidence (Gramm, 1986) suggests that the propensity to strike is lower in small bargaining units than large ones—Kaufman's data are liable to exert a positive bias on the coefficient associated with the negotiations measure (Gramm, 1987, p. 2). Roomkin (1976) faces similar problems. The data discrepancies encountered by Roomkin and Kaufman occur because the individual contract negotiation is not the same unit of analysis in the compilation of the strike data. Gramm's measure of strike propensity is more precise because it is derived from a single sample of negotiations in which strike incidence is observed for each case.

Using Gramm's sample of collective bargaining negotiations for over 200 manufacturing firm-and-union pairs in the 1971-1980 period, I will analyze strike activity by conducting a detailed probit analysis of both defensive and aggressive intercontractual strike propensity. These two probit models will be constructed to investigate the conditional probability of a strike's occurrence during contract negotiations, given the hypothesized explanatory variables.

As indicated earlier, it would also be desirable to include a more refined study that analyses aggressive and defensive separately for wage and non-wage strikes respectively. Unfortunately, because of the limited scope of Gramm's data set, an additional refinement that breaks down strikes into wage and non-wage strikes is not possible. (See appendix B for a full description of the data sets used.)

C. The Determinants of Strike Activity.

A set of variables outlining the relative power of capitalists and workers is proposed as the general model for the analysis of defensive and aggressive strikes. This approach, based on Marxian political economic theory, takes as its starting point the relative structural and institutional power of labor and capital.

According to the Marxian framework, unions are created and influenced by the intrinsic conflict between capitalists and workers; unions are workers' mechanisms for seeking protection from capitalists' power. Best enunciated by Gordon (1981) and Hyman (1975), this approach locates the origin and function of unions in the social relations of capitalist production. Capitalists have a class monopoly over the means of production and workers are a class of wage-earners who sell their capacity to work. According to Marxian theory, workers, as part of the wage bargain in capitalism, give up control over their labor during the working day and have little say in the disposition of the things they produce. Capitalists use their power over the production process to profit from the labor of workers. Workers, as a result, are continually forced to take actions which will augment their relative power to increase their wages and improve their working conditions. The institutionalization of unions has its roots in this inherent struggle, called the class struggle, between capitalists and workers.

I will include in my analysis many economic variables that condition the class struggle and that set the context for fluctuations in industrial relations. More specifically, the variables in this approach will be operationalized for: 1. a discriminant analysis that will divide defensive and aggressive wage strikes; 2. two probit procedures that will separately analyze the conditions surrounding aggressive and defensive strike propensity at the bargaining unit of analysis. In this section, I outline a number of discrete hypotheses about the influence of several variables on aggressive and defensive strikes. Table 1 lists these variables along with their sign expectations to which subsequent discussion makes reference. Appendix A details the data construction and the data sources.

1. Capitalist Strength

According to Marxian political economic theory, capitalists derive their power from the fact that they own the means of production. Individual capitalists control the workplace at the point of production, and, collectively, capitalists determine the fate of the economy through their individual decisions on investment. Capitalists use these forms of power to create conditions favorable to their own interests.

> If the constituent institutions of the social structure of accumulation are stable . . . capitalists are likely to feel secure about investing in the expansion of productive capacity. But if the social structure begins to become shaky . . . capitalists will be more inclined to put their money in financial rather than direct investments . . . (Gordon et al. 1982, p. 263).

When conditions are unfavorable for corporate profitability, capitalists tend to speculate rather than invest productively, precipitating an economic crisis. When profitability improves, capitalists again invest and the economy pulls out of the crisis. The ability of capitalists to make profit depends on their power over labor. I detail below the factors that would be likely to condition management's power and correspondingly influence the incidence of aggressive and defensive strikes.

A. Economic Blackmail—The Unemployment Rate.

In the late 1960s and early 1970s, U.S. capitalism confronted a crisis; continued growth and low unemployment entailed a deterioration in workplace control and lower profit rates. Any restoration of profit rates required that labor be more vulnerable to the threat of high unemployment and economic insecurity. Consequently, workers'

Table 1

Dimensions of the Capital-Labor Balance of Power as Determinants of Strike Activity
(with sign expectations)

	Aggressive Strikes	Defensive Strikes
Capitalist Strength		
1. State Unemployment Rate (UN)	–	+
2. The Injury Rate (INJ)	+	+
3. Unfair Labor Practices (UF)	–	+
Worker Strength		
1. State or Regional Unionization Rate (SU)	+	+
2. Proportion of Unionized Workers in Industry who are Male (PM)	+	+
3. Proportion of Unionized Workers in Industry who are White (PW)	+	+
4. Relative Wage of White to Black Unionized Workers in Industry (UW)	–	–
5. Relative Wage of Male to Female Unionized Workers in Industry (UM)	–	–
6. Ratio of Quits to Layoffs (QL)	+	–
Worker Expectations		
1. Ratio of Percent Change in Nominal Wage to Percent Change in CPI in Previous Contract (EX)	–	–
Capitalist Economic Vulnerability		
1. Coefficient of Variation in Shipments (SH)	+	–
2. Percentage Change in New Orders the Year Preceeding Negotiations (PN)	+	–
3. Percent of the Previous Years New Orders Recieved the Quarter before Negotiations (NO)	+	–
4. Ratio Labor Costs to Value Added in Industry (LC)	+	?
5. Proportion of Indusrty Workers who are Non-Supervisory (NS)	+	?
Worker Economic Vulnerability		
1. Annual Percentage Change in the Cost of Job Loss (CJL)	–	+
Controls		
1. Business Cycle (BC)	–	+
2. Wage-Price Controls (C)	–	–
3. Interaction (BC*UN)	–	?
4. 8 Firm Concentration Ratio	+	?

resistance and the consequent deterioration in corporate profits led to a restrictive fiscal policy and lower levels of business investment. Individual capitalists launched a capital strike by reducing investments or not investing at all.[1] It is hypothesized that the high levels of unemployment and underutilized capacity that resulted were, therefore, attributable at least in part to capital's attempts to discipline labor and forge a favorable economic climate.

I hypothesize, therefore, that unemployment is an important measure of capitalists' relative power vis a vis labor because capitalists control access to jobs and workers need jobs to survive (Bowles et al., 1989, p. 115). Tight labor markets render capital vulnerable to labor's demands and slack labor markets reflect capital's struggle to discipline labor with the threat of dismissal. It is therefore hypothesized that workers will be likely to strike in a defensive manner in response to management aggression at those times when workers face a high degree of unemployment.[2] Obversely, I hypothesize that workers will strike in an aggressive manner when the labor market improves and labor is in a better bargaining position.

In an aggregate, time series analysis that excludes wage strikes, Michele Naples (1987) concludes that defensive strikes are positively related to unemployment in the postwar era (1953-1981). Her analysis also provides evidence that all other strikes are negatively related to unemployment. Although her study suffers from many of the same weaknesses of recent strike studies (she doesn't control for strike opportunity and she fails to include many important variables indicative of the balance of power between labor and management), Naples offers the first serious empirical analysis of defensive strikes that, at least, points to the pressing need for a further elaboration of the relationship between labor market conditions and defensive strike activity.

Most other studies mirror Gramm's approach (1982); they incorporate the unemployment rate as a measure of the employer's ability to continue operations during a strike. According to Gramm, high unemployment facilitates uninterrupted operations by assuring a supply of laborers who are readily available to replace striking workers. In contrast, the employer's ability to maintain market share deteriorates as unemployment falls and as it becomes harder to replace workers and maintain production. While this general labor market analysis is not inconsistent with my approach, Gramm's analysis does not explicitly acknowledge the influence of market conditions on an authority relationship at the workplace that is an inherent axis of contention between labor and management.

Along with other mainstream approaches, Gramm's analysis suffers from a lack of appreciation of the intrinsic power struggle that is at the heart of the history of class relations. Most theorists like Gramm confine their models to an analysis of unemployment within a cost-benefit approach of economic gains and losses. However, such approaches can make little sense of at least strike activity since they fail to account for strikes that occur even in the face of defeat for one of the combatants—a strategy in which the ongoing class struggle is about, rather than within the rules of the game—when one party defends its established prerogatives in the face of what it perceives as an aggressive assault by the other party.[3] Strike activity in the 1970's appears to have followed this pattern; they were more than just struggles over immediate short-term goals. On the contrary, I hypothesize that they represented an outbreak of class warfare over long term institutional practices; they were a fight over the establishment of new forms of regularized behavior in labor-management relations.[4]

In order to test my hypothesis about the differential effect of unemployment, I will use Gramm's estimate of the unemployment rate by state or region of the bargaining unit for the month under consideration (UN) for the statistical procedures in the analysis.[5]

B. Management Aggression—The Injury Rate and Unfair Labor Practices.

Jens Christiansen has shown that different strike patterns in the U.S. and West German Steel industry are at least in part attributable to differences in the underlying stability of the collective bargaining relationship (Christiansen, 1982). Two measures will be used as proxies for management's attempts to subvert the collective bargaining relationship and disrupt the capital-labor accord: the industrial injury rate and unfair labor practices.

The Injury Rate. As management becomes more aggressive, cutting corners in an attempt to increase productivity, the industrial accident rate should increase. Naples (1986) has argued that managerial efforts to increase the efficiency and intensity of labor explain the secular increase in the injury rate in the 1960s and 1970s.

Figure 4 shows that the injury frequency rate in manufacturing reached its lowest point since 1926 in the early 1960s when the capital-labor accord was fully in place and consolidated. The accord began to unravel in the mid 1960s as management began to press workers on the shop floor. As a consequence, she argues, the injury rate accelerated in the late 1960s and steadily increased at about a 5 percent annual rate through 1979. Peter Arno (1982) uses a similar approach in his analysis of the pattern of industrial injuries in the United States in the postwar period.

I hypothesize that workers, faced with management aggression in the workplace, have no choice but to react. Increasing accidents undermine workers' commitment to industrial peace and the capital-labor accord. The increase in workers' discontent documented by Staines (1979) should be in part due to the increases in the injury rate. In fact, Staines' measure of worker dissatisfaction mirrors the

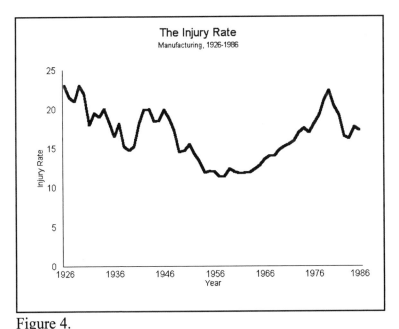

Figure 4.
Source: Arno, Peter, "The Political Economy of Industrial Injuries," unpublished PH.D dissertation, 1984.

industry rate, increasing between 1969 and 1973, and accelerating between 1973 and 1977.

In general, a deterioration in workplace safety should have a positive effect on both defensive and aggressive strike propensity as workers' overall discontent escalates: workers will not feel prevented by the terms of a deteriorating accord from acting aggressively to improve working conditions and they will be forced to defend themselves in the face of other management aggressions that the injury rate reflects. Increases in the injury rate, INJ, therefore, will be interpreted as reflecting a soured relationship in which the struggle between labor and capital intensifies.

Unfortunately, the BLS changed its method for collecting and calculating the injury rate in 1971, thereby creating two discontinuous time series. Following Peter Arno's "splicing" method (1982), I create a consistent times series for the 1970s for all two-digit manufacturing industries. This allows me to consider lagged values of the injury rate in my statistical tests.

Unfair Labor Practices. Another measure of the underlying health of the collective bargaining relationship is the number of complaints filed with the National Labor Relations Board under Section 8 of the Labor Management Relations act. Unfair labor practice charges filed under section 8(CA) consist of complaints by workers or unions against employers usually during the renegotiation of an existing contract. Like Byrne and King (1986), I hypothesize that "if the relationship is strained, the probability of a charge being filed will increase" (Bryne and King, 1986., p. 392). The number of charges filed as a percentage of unionized workers, UF, will be used as a proxy for a deteriorated relationship that is eventuated by management aggression.

The form of management aggression that UF captures is certainly different than INJ: INJ deals with conditions on the shop floor, while UF deals more directly with the stability of the renegotiating process. The postwar capital-labor accord set the contours of the collective bargaining process—negotiations centered mainly around wage increases and fringe benefits with management having secured its prerogatives to control freely the administration and conditions of work and labor, in return, having secured, among other things, a degree of job security. It is proposed here that management is most aggressive, precipitating unfair labor charges, during negotiations when labor is relatively weak: a large number of unfair labor practices reflects labor's weakness and management's willingness to pursue its advantage. In such cases, one recourse for labor is to defend itself with a strike. Consequently, the greater the number of unfair labor practices, the greater the number of defensive strikes and the fewer the number of aggressive strikes. The source of these data was yearly issues of the *Annual Report of the National Labor Relations Board.*

2. Workers' Strength

Again following Marxian theory, the struggles of workers against capitalists arise from the antagonistic nature of the relationship between capitalists and workers in the capitalist mode of production. The lack of freedom and equality that characterizes the capitalist labor process sets the context for a continuous struggle between capital and labor over wages, job security and the intensity and conditions of work. As Richard Hyman has observed:

> . . . within the workplace itself, the wage labor relationship contains a constant potential for disorder. Management commands, employees are expected to obey; but the limits of management authority and worker obedience are imprecise and shifting. The frontier of control . . . must be constantly negotiated through a permanent process of pressure and counter pressure, the mobilization of both sides of sanctions and resources, at the point of production (1975, p. 25).

Workers organize and join unions to increase their strength in bargaining with capitalists. Through trade unions, a formal basis is consolidated as a countervailing institution of control, which resists and, at times, neutralizes the dominance of the employer. The most overt expression of workers' resistance and power is the collective withholding of labor power: the strike. At the point of production, strikes are the most accessible and powerful means by which workers can challenge capitalists. Engels perceived the significance of the early forms of collective action by British workers in the 1840s:

What gives these Unions and the strikes arising from them their real
significance is this, that they are the first attempt of the workers to
abolish competition. They imply the recognition of the fact that
supremacy of the bourgeoisie is based wholly on the competition of
the workers among themselves; i.e. upon their want of cohesion.
And precisely because Unions direct themselves against the vital
nerve of the present social order, however onesidedly, in however
a narrow way, are they so dangerous to this social order. The
working-men cannot attack the bourgeoisie, and with it the whole
existing order of society, at any sorer point than this (1978, p. 683).

For the remainder of this section, I will analyze the internal
dimensions of union structure and behavior that condition strike
activity.

A. Institutional Strength.

It is hypothesized that the very fact of union membership itself
influences industrial conflict positively on the expectation that 1)
increased economic leverage, worker solidarity, ability to outlast
employer resistance and calculations of success probabilities all
characterize stronger labor organizations and 2) given these actual and
perceived power advantages, labor is better able and more likely to
press its collective demands in work stoppages. The risk of
replacement should be low in communities where organizational
strength runs high and the risk of "scabbing" is diminished.
Organizational strength is an institutional prerequisite for all types of
strikes, whether workers are aggressively making new demands or
defensively responding to management hostility. Many studies show
that total strike activity is significantly influenced by union density at
the national, state or industry level (Snyder, 1977; Edwards, 1977;
Kaufman, 1988; and Gramm, 1986).

Following Gramm, I measure union organizational strength as the
percent of the total labor force that is unionized in the state or region
in which the unit is located, SU. This measure should be positively
related to both defensive and aggressive strike activity.

Union organizational strength and strikes are further mediated by
the solidarity and relative strength of rank-and-file activity within a

union. A severely divided membership, no matter its size, is in a weak position to conduct effective strikes. Again, it is assumed that a divided union is not in a position to act aggressively nor institutionally capable of responding to management aggression. It is crucial, therefore, to include indicators of internal union cohesiveness and strength in any model of strike activity. Two potential divisions are of particular importance to union strength: sexual and racial discrimination.

As already mentioned, unions are a method for overcoming competition and uniting workers. Discrimination, in contrast, tends to stimulate and reproduce divisions among workers. Michael Reich (1982) has pointed out that capitalists have not invented discrimination or racism, but have used preexisting prejudices to divide and weaken workers:

> While racism continues to divide workers, it is not created solely or even primarily today by the conscious effort of capitalists to trick their workers. The racism of whites is being reinforced today by the insecurities created by the decline of the American economy, by the decline of individual autonomy in craft and professional occupations, by the strains that effect family structure and by the increase of individualism in our culture. In this context, racist appeals and responses can and do appear attractive to broad segments of the white population. (Reich, 1982, p. 312)

One of the most effective means for capitalists to foster divisions between workers is to segregate jobs by race and sex (Foner, 1974; Gordon, Edwards and Reich, 1982; Hogan, 1984). The best paid workers (white and male) fear being paid like the lowest paid workers (blacks and women) and resist efforts to fight for racial and sexual equality in job assignments. In this context, racist and sexist appeals find a strong echo; racism and sexism provide vulnerable scapegoats upon whom the frustrations of capitalism can be directed. As a result, the working class is divided and less able to fight for its collective benefit against capitalists.

Ideally, information on the union workers involved in a strike should be utilized. However, these data are unavailable and the best alternative data is for data on workers in the same industry. On this basis, I have constructed two approximate measures of the debilitating divisions and tensions that result from gender and racial prejudice. The first proxy is PM, the proportion of unionized workers in the bargaining unit's industry who are male and the second is PW, the proportion of unionized workers who are white. It is hypothesized that a diverse workforce inflames racial and sexual prejudices and that a more sexually and racially uniform workforce is in a better position to act collectively. Therefore, on this basis, PM and PW are expected to be positively related to a workforce's ability and willingness to conduct defensive and aggressive strikes.

It is not enough, however, to reduce racial and sexual tension to the prior existence of racial prejudice. Whites and males may believe that they gain materially at the expense of blacks and women by reserving the best jobs for themselves. I hypothesize that where jobs are segregated, whites and males are reluctant to unite with blacks and women for fear of reducing their job status and being paid like blacks and women. In the following analysis, UW, the relative wages of whites to blacks for unionized, full-time workers in a given industry and, UM, the relative wages of males to females for unionized full-time workers, will act as proxies for job segregation by race and sex. It is assumed that wage differentials are a result of job segregation and not pay discrimination—paying one group of workers less than another for the same job. This is not an extraordinary assumption since studies have shown that the union policy of "equal pay for equal work" has greatly reduced pay discrimination in the core industries under investigation.[6] It is, therefore, hypothesized that job segregation by race and sex, whether initiated by the union or management, creates competitive tension among workers in a union and weakens its ability to conduct both defensive and aggressive strikes.[7] The data for this section are taken from the U.S. Department of Labor, Bureau of Labor Statistics, *Current Population Survey, May, 1969-1981*.

B. Individual Actions.

Quit frequencies reflect a combination of job dissatisfaction and workers sense of independence from their employers. Satisfied workers may not quit their jobs even if they have a sense of independence. I hypothesize that workers will quit, however, when they are dissatisfied and feel that they are in an economic position to leave. In the 1960s and early 1970s, when workers began to take advantage of reduced corporate leverage, it is reasonable to assume that their collective actions mirrored their individual ones, reflecting a situation in which workers were increasingly dissatisfied with their jobs and more willing to act in accordance with their discontent. I hypothesize that during the economic decline of the mid 1970s, workers, dissatisfied but fearing layoffs, were in less a position to act independently. Increasingly less powerful, workers protected themselves with collective action in the form of defensive strikes, instead of quitting and looking for better jobs. My hypothesis about the meaning of quits closely follows the approach suggested by Bowles et al. (1984, p. 90):

> Workers may quit because they hate their work or their boss, or simply because they have a good prospect of finding a boss, or simply because they have a good prospect of finding a better job, do not expect to remain unemployed for long, and have something to live on while they wait. Quit frequencies, as a result reflect either job resistance or workers' sense of independence . . . Layoffs, on the other hand, are imposed upon workers by their employers; layoffs inflict considerable losses on some workers and tend to place workers on the defensive.[8]

I measure the ability and willingness of workers to act independently by the ratio of quits to layoffs, QL. I hypothesize that QL is positively related to the incidence of aggressive strikes and inversely related to defensive strikes. The source for this variable was the U.S. Department of Labor, Bureau of Labor Statistics, *Employment and Earnings, United States, 1909-78* and annual publications of the March issue of *Employment and Earnings* for the years 1979 to 1981.[9]

3. Workers' Expectations.

Rank-and-file activity depends on the degree to which their expectations are fulfilled. If due either to inaccurate forecasts or to the existence of long term contracts, union members find that their real wages have grown less than expected, their nominal wage demands will increase in the next period, not only to restore a desired level of real wages but also to restore the loss in real wages suffered in the previous contract. To paraphrase James Davies (1969, p. 162), collective action is more likely to take place when a prolonged period of rising expectations and rising gratifications is followed by a period during which the gap between expectations and gratifications widens.

The high inflation rates of the 1970's created systematic deviations between anticipated and actual price increases, forcing workers to ask for more in nominal wages than they would have in the absence of inflation. It is assumed that this had a disruptive influence on collective bargaining, straining an already fragile capital-labor accord that was not fully equipped to deal with high inflation rates.[10] The approach taken here hypothesizes that inflation in the 1970s increased workers' demands to make up for past losses and heightened uncertainty about future price levels. This increased the likelihood that management and labor would disagree over future wage levels. As a consequence, workers began to lose faith in a collective bargaining process that potentially eroded their real wages; therefore, they became more willing to strike over any issue. On the other side, as inflation potentially reduced their future profits in the form of higher worker wages, management became more recalcitrant in its demands.

Inflation creates tension in labor-management relations over future prices and past real wage losses. This dynamic is captured in this study with the ratio of the percentage change in the nominal wage to the percentage change in the consumer price index, EX, over the term of the previous contract. This ratio controls for the change in money wages and, as such, should capture past unanticipated inflation. It is expected to be inversely related to all types of strike activity, defensive and aggressive.[11]

Finally, I also control for the effects of the Nixon wage-price controls, using a variable, C, suggested by Robert Gordon (1982). I anticipate a negative relationship, other things equal, between the wage-price controls and both defensive and aggressive strikes—assuming that stable prices lead to less uncertainty during collective bargaining, which, in turn, decreases the likelihood of a strike eruption.

4. Economic Context of Class Relations.

In any bargaining situation, the costs to each party of terminating the relationship are a strong determinant of the outcome. Any decision by workers or management to initiate a strike includes an assessment of the probability of winning, as partially determined by their ability to impose greater economic costs on their negotiating adversary than themselves. The function of a strike is to increase the costs of disagreement for the other side until they find it advantageous to compromise.

The business cycle provides one important general economic context in which strike activity fluctuates between worker initiated, aggressive strikes and management initiated, defensive strikes. During deteriorating economic times, management power is relatively enhanced: workers find themselves increasingly vulnerable to severe economic conditions and management, facing low profitability and decreased demand, seeks to cut costs by antagonizing workers and trying to take back previous union gains. In contrast, during economic upswings, conditions are more propitious for labor to take aggressive actions and make new demands on management. In this case, management is more vulnerable economically, making strikes more costly for it to bear. I include below a number of variables that reflect the economic costs imposed on the parties involved in a breakdown of negotiations. To control for the effects of the business cycle not captured by these specific variables, I include a dummy variable for the business cycle, BC and an interaction term, INT, between BC and UN, the unemployment rate.

BC takes on a value of 0 for the business cycle upswing and value 1 for the downswing. It stands to reason that aggressive strikes will occur during the upswing and should, therefore, be inversely related to BC while defensive strikes, occurring during the downswing, should be directly related to it.

The interaction term, included to capture the interactive effects of the business cycle and the unemployment rate, should be negative for aggressive strikes since these strikes occur during the upswing when, by design, the interaction term takes on the value of zero. In addition, as the economy worsens during the downswing and INT increases, the number of aggressive strikes should diminish.

By contrast, INT may have either a positive or negative effect on defensive strike incidence. In one direction, during the downswing when defensive strikes should happen, increases in unemployment may, after a certain point, decrease the likelihood of a defensive strike. Here, defensive strikes may occur when the unemployment rate is generally high, but as it increases, workers will become so vulnerable to layoffs and dismissal that, despite management aggression, workers will forgo all defensive strike activity. In the other direction, as unemployment worsens during the downswings and management becomes increasingly more aggressive, unionized workers, *ceteris paribus*, will protect themselves with more defensive strikes even in the face of imminent defeat.

A. Management's Economic Vulnerability.

The costs felt by the employers during a strike will depend on their ability to retain market shares and the ease with which strikers may be replaced or other sources of product supply secured during a strike. A number of variables will be included as indicators of the costumers a capitalist risks losing during a strike.

I assume that capitalists stand to lose more customers when there is a greater the demand for timely deliveries. Therefore, the capitalist's ability to retain its market share during a strike is expected to vary inversely with the coefficient of variation in shipments for the year preceding the strike, SH. SH, in this case, acts as an indicator of the variability of customer demand for timely deliveries. Similarly, in an expanding market, reflected by the percentage change in new orders over the year ending the month preceding the negotiation, PN, the employer forfeits the opportunity to add new customers. A third measure, NO, the percent of the previous year's new orders that were received during the quarter ending the month preceding the strike, indicates whether the contract expiration coincides with a season of high demand when the loss of customers due to a strike would be higher than in seasons with low demand. Under the assumption that a strike is instigated by either party in the class struggle, it is reasonable to assume that labor will engage in more aggressive strikes when capital is vulnerable, that is, when SH, PN and NO are all high. Conversely, capital will push labor out on defensive strikes when any or all three of these indicators are stagnant. All three variables are measured at the industry unit of analysis and were made available by Cynthia Gramm.

The ease of maintaining production is more complex to model. I will assume that labor intensive operations are likely to be slowed or halted while highly automated production facilities, using a skeletal staff, are likely to operate more easily during a strike. The ratio of labor costs to value added for the unit's industry, LC, represents the ability of the employer to maintain operations during a strike. The less labor intensive an industry, *ceteris paribus*, the less likely workers will engage in aggressive strikes because of management's increased strength. In contrast, management, recognizing its strength, will press labor into defensive strikes when it becomes increasingly easy to maintain production during a potential strike. Therefore, it would seem reasonable that the less labor intensive an industry, the greater the number of defensive strikes. However, it is hard to make such a hypothesis with any degree of certainty since workers, beyond a certain point, will not be in a position to strike at all because of their radically reduced numbers and diminished strength. LC, in this case, simultaneously and directly captures labor's institutional vulnerability. Therefore, the overall effect of LC on defensive strikes is theoretically indeterminate. This variable was constructed at the industry level of analysis using the BLS *Current Population Survey*.

Another measure, the proportion of workers in a unit's industry who are employed in non-supervisory production and service jobs, NS, also reflects an employer's ability to continue production during a strike. Workers in professional, managerial and technical occupations, being more unorganized than their coworkers in production and maintenance occupations, are unlikely to support their unionized coworkers during a strike. NS, therefore, captures the degree of employee division within an industry and, as such, acts as an indicator of an employer's ability to continue production with the assistance of non-union, supervisory workers. On the basis of this assumption, NS should be positively related to aggressive strikes on the expectation that a greater proportion of production and maintenance workers reflects a greater cohesiveness among workers which, in turn, makes it more difficult for employers to maintain production during a strike. However, like LC, the relationship between management's ability to maintain production and defensive strikes is theoretically ambiguous. Therefore, it is hypothesized that the direction of influence of NS on defensive strikes, as with LC, is theoretically indeterminate. Once again this variable was constructed using data from the 1973-1975 *Current Population Survey*.

B. Workers' Economic Vulnerability

As already indicated, the unemployment rate by state is used as a measure of job security and the degree of competition for jobs. Bowles and Schor (1986) have provided evidence that the cost of job loss acts as a complementary measure of the relative power of capital and labor. Bowles and Schor construct the cost of job loss as a combination of unemployment duration and the proportion of income foregone when workers loose their jobs. When the cost of job loss is high, workers face economic hardships in the form of extensive unemployment duration and lost income. As Bowles and Schor state:

> The cost of job loss is the hypothetical difference between the worker's expected income with and without a spell of unemployment defined arbitrarily over the period of one year. It is based on the situation of a composite employed worker relative to the same worker if unemployed. We have created this composite worker by calculating various combinations of social welfare benefits, program eligibility and reemployment wage rate loss and weighting these combinations by the labor force composition of the group to which they correspond (Bowles and Schor, 1986, p. 3).[12]

When workers' resources are limited, management is in a better position to antagonize workers and to try to eliminate previous gains by labor. Not only are workers weaker when the cost of job loss is high, but firms also anticipate less of a reduction in market share during a strike in such a period because demand is simultaneously low. Therefore, it is hypothesized that an increase in the annual percentage change in the cost of job loss, CJL, should lead to more defensive strikes as labor defends itself against management aggressions. For the same reasons, when the cost of job loss is low, workers are better able to resist the demands of management and can impose greater costs on them during a strike. In such a situation, labor can bargain more effectively for higher wages and better working conditions. Therefore, it stands to reason that a negative CJL leads to a greater number of aggressive strikes. This variable was generously provided by Thomas E. Weisskopf and is measured at the three digit SIC level of analysis.

D. Summary

The balance of power between labor and management establishes the conditions that precipitate open hostilities in the form of strikes. In this study, I detail the state of industrial relations surrounding two very different sorts of strikes: aggressive and defensive. I hypothesize that the relations of production differ substantially between these two types of strikes: aggressive strikes occur when labor is stronger than those times when, in contrast, labor, facing a more powerful adversary, is forced into defensive strikes. I use many key variables to capture the state of industrial relations surrounding aggressive and defensive strikes. These variables are intended to capture the state of the class struggle and are inclusive of economic, institutional and political conditions.

NOTES

1. Econometric evidence to support this interpretation is given in Bowles et al. (1984).

2. As far back as 1921, Hansen suggested that when conditions are to labor's disadvantage, most strikes will be defensive and counter-cyclical.

3. Shorter and Tilly state, "The outcomes of French strikes have been so dismal over the years, and their growing lack of success so palpable, that one wonders why the workers bothered" (1974, p. 64).

4. For a similar explanation of this methodology, see Robert Franzosi (1989).

5. Because monthly state unemployment rates are not available for the 1970s, I will use Gramm's approximate measure. See Appendix A for details of data.

6. According to Freeman and Medoff (1984) the factor determining the union wage effect on demographic groups doing the same job is the standard rate pay policies of unions. These policies require companies to give equal pay for equal work to workers within a firm and across industries, denying management the ability to set pay on a case by case basis. Their empirical data show that union establishments average one-third less inequality than non-union establishments.

7. A number of studies include percentage males and/or percentage whites at the industrial unit of analysis (see Gramm, 1986; Tracy, 1987; Bryne and King, 1986 and Gramm et al., 1988; Godard, 1992). Most of these studies assume that these measures are indicative of the individual characteristics that these different groups bring to the process of collective bargaining. For instance, Gramm (1986) and Kaufman (1983) offer the hypothesis that women have a more sympathetic relationship towards management than men, that women are less militant. Godard (1992) assumes that women are more inclined to quit than go out on strike. Other studies assume that these measures are indicative of the different types of jobs in which these groups tend to be concentrated. Byrne and King (1986) assume that women tend to be concentrated in jobs that have less onerous working environments and Gramm (1986) hypothesizes that women's segregation into low wage jobs enhances the attractiveness of nonmarket work. All of these approaches are not sensitive enough to the historical context of the power struggle between labor and capital—they ignore racism and its effects on workers' ability to act collectively. I would argue that a more thorough approach situates differences among workers within the class struggle and analyses the effects of these differences on workers ability to act collectively.

8. One of the few strike studies that explicitly theorizes the relationship between quits and strike activity is offered by John Godard (1992). For Godard (p. 163), "to the extent that quitting is viable, discontented workers are more likely to choose this option, hence reducing the likelihood of a strike." Unfortunately, Godard gives no strong reason to consider strikes and quits as substitutes and he doesn't directly test his approach empirically. Rather, he utilizes his proposition on quits to hypothesize the relationship between other variables and strike activity. For instance he assumes that the percentage of females to be negatively associated with strikes on the assumption that women have a higher propensity to exit than man and hence view exit as more effective than striking. In this case, his empirical results are inconclusive. In another approach, Bowles et al. (1984) show that the

percentage of workers involved in strikes follows the ratio of the quits to layoff very closely. However, they don't test the correlation econometrically.

9. These data were generously provided by Bruce Pietrykowski.

10. During the 1970s, the capital-labor accord was only partially successful in decreasing the effects of inflation on strike activity with the inclusion of cost of living adjustments in 36% of all contracts in 1975 (BNA, 1975). Furthermore, Henry Farber (1977) found that COLAS offset only 40% of price changes in the 1970s (the extent to which COLA clauses provided protection from inflation depended on the formula for converting price changes to wage changes and the benefits covered). Nevertheless, two studies, Gramm (1988) and Kaufman (1981) found evidence that COLAS indeed serve in part to eliminate the effects of inflation on price expectations as well as on catch-up wage demands.

11. Kaufman shows that inflation is important in explaining all strikes, economic and non-economic: ". . . within American manufacturing the most important cause for the recent increase in strikes has been the disrupting influence of inflation on collective bargaining" (1981, p.353).

12. The annual 'cost of job loss' has been estimated and used to explain the aggregate slowdown in U.S. productivity growth (Weisskopf, Bowles and Gordon, 1983) and profitability (Bowles, Gordon and Weisskopf, 1986) and time series variations in strike activity (Bowles and Schor, 1986). For a more detailed discussion of the construction of the variable, please see appendix A.

CHAPTER V

Identifying Defensive and Aggressive Strikes

I classify here all strikes in the 1970s as either defensive or aggressive. I first classify many non-wage strikes according to the issue of contention and I then classify wage strikes on the basis of a discriminant analysis which differentiates between aggressive and defensive wage strikes by assuming that the conditions surrounding wage strikes are analogous to those surrounding non-wage strikes. Finally, the discriminant analysis allows me to examine whether aggressive and defensive strikes occurred under different conditions in the 1970s.

A. Non-Wage Strikes

Data collected by the Bureau of Labor Statistics on strikes in the 1970's for the manufacturing sector detail the issue involved for every strike that involves six or more workers.[1] Using the history of postwar industrial relations as a guide, I categorize non-wage strikes as aggressive or defensive according to the issues recorded by the BLS.

During the inception of the truce between labor and management, organized labor was able to force upon management a system that limited management's discretion in the allocation of labor: jobs were finely divided within internal promotional systems and along detailed job ladders. As Richard Edwards emphasizes, "labor management came more and more to rely on the logic and operations of a full set of rules and procedures rather than the direct and haphazard intervention of the supervisor's authority" (1979, p. 131). In the 1970s workers went out on strike on a number of occasions to maintain these previously achieved gains. The Bureau of Labor Statistics identifies three strike issues that are particularly relevant: seniority and/or layoffs and the division of work. I define any strike over these three issues as defensive.

For its part, management benefited from the truce to the extent that it obtained a relatively free hand in the administration of the shop floor and realized a degree of industrial peace. In the postwar era disruptive forms of industrial conflict were institutionally redirected toward negotiations and grievance procedures. I consider any strike that clearly encroaches upon management's accustomed prerogatives and bypasses negotiations and grievance procedures as aggressive. The BLS recognizes four types of strikes that seem representative of labor's attempts assertively to step outside the boundaries of the truce to address its grievances: strikes over physical shop conditions and strikes over insubordination, discharge and disciplinary suspension. Included in strikes over shop conditions are disputes over temperature and dangerous equipment or surroundings. These strikes go to the heart of management's accustomed control over working conditions.[2] Strikes over "discharge, disciplinary suspension, and insubordination" are particularly pertinent. In 1975, over 90% of all contracts had discharge and discipline provisions that gave management the right to discipline and fire workers for very specific reasons, including insubordination.[3] All of these contracts detailed the procedures involved for workers interested in filing a grievance in response to a discharge or suspension. Resolution of such conflicts were usually based on formal juridical principles that culminated in a decision by an "impartial" arbitrator. By bypassing grievance procedures or ignoring arbitration decisions with a strike, workers aggressively violated the formalized relationship that was institutionalized in the capital-labor accord: they were aggressive on the job, violating specific work rules of plant management, and they aggressively disregarded grievance procedures and went on strike to protect that behavior. For these reasons, I consider non-wage strikes over physical shop conditions, insubordination, discharge and disciplinary suspension as aggressive.

The postwar capital-labor accord that directed industrial conflict away from strikes was relatively successful until 1965-66, when strikes escalated and the postwar labor peace began to deteriorate. During the late 1960s and the 1970s, strikes increased as labor and management challenged the traditional rules of the postwar truce. Strikes erupted when the conflict was about, rather than within, the rules of the accord. This period was characterized by an accelerated struggle to reconstitute postwar industrial relations and included a number of strikes over wages.[4]

Unfortunately, I only was able to classify around 30% of all non-wage issues identified by the BLS. The BLS identifies roughly 30% of such strikes as "other" and the remaining 40% fall under two broad categories that cannot be easily identified as defensive or aggressive: interunion or intraunion matters (like jurisdiction over the representation of workers) and union organization or recognition (like certification or the vaguely worded "strengthening of bargaining position"). These unclassified strikes were subsequently divided along with wage strikes in the discriminant analysis.

The BLS data set does not detail the objects of wage strikes, providing information only on whether the issue was a general wage increase or general wage decrease. Without information on the exact level of wages in contention, it is not possible to compare wage demands to inflation and productivity growth. Therefore, it cannot be determined whether the wage issue is within the confines of the annual improvement factor (AIF) stipulated by the capital-labor accord.[5] However, as noted earlier, I assume that wage and non-wage strikes exhibit similar patterns and shifts in bargaining power. Consequently, I use discriminant analysis to distinguish between defensive and aggressive wage strikes on the basis of the issues of known non-wage strikes.

B. Wage Strikes—Discriminant Analysis

Discriminant analysis is a statistical procedure that predicts group membership for unknown cases on the basis of the group characteristics of known cases (Norusis 1988; Aldrich and Nelson, 1984). Using discriminant analysis, a linear combination of bargaining power variables will be formed on the basis of the available data on non-wage strikes and then utilized as a discriminant benchmark for classifying wage strikes. The linear equation, called a "canonical discriminant function," is similar to the multiple linear regression equation and has the following mathematical form:

$$f_{km} = u_0 + u_1 X_{1km} + u_2 X_{2km} + \ldots u_p X_{pkm}$$

where f_{km} = the value of the canonical discriminant function for case m in group k;
X_{ikm} = the value of the discriminating variable X_i for case m in group k; and
u_i = linear coefficients representing the association between X_{ikm} and f_{km}.

If a linear discriminant function is to distinguish between defensive and aggressive strikes, the two groups must differ in their discriminant function values. Therefore, the coefficients (u_i) are chosen so that the values of the discriminant function differ as much as possible between the groups. Discriminant analysis achieves this result by maximizing the ratio of the between-groups sum of squares and the within-groups sum of squares. Any other linear combination of the discriminant variables will have a smaller ratio.

Once a discriminant score is calculated for all strikes, a common technique, called Bayes' rule, uses the discriminant score for classifying unknown strikes as either aggressive or defensive. Bayes' rules assumes that the discriminant scores for strikes in each of the two groups are normally distributed and that the parameters of this distribution mirror the parameters of the discriminant scores for the known strikes. On this basis, Bayes' rule classifies a strike to the group in which it has the highest probability of belonging.

1. Discriminant Variables

The discriminant variables define the group characteristics that allow for the classification of a strike into the group that it most closely resembles. In the following section I will define the discriminant variables and their expected contribution to the discriminant function. Once the function is estimated, I will then use several statistical procedures to test the hypothesized expectations about the power of the variables to discriminate between defensive and aggressive strikes. With few exceptions, the discriminating variables are the same as the power variables outlined in chapter four and are used on similar theoretical grounds.

Capitalist Strength

Capacity Utilization

Following Bowles, Gordon and Weisskopf (1986), I use capacity utilization as a measure at least partly of capitalist power: "over the relevant range of economic activity and public policy, given an existing institutional framework, the elements of capitalist power may be increased but only at the expense of movements in capacity utilization adversely affecting either profits or accumulation" (Bowles et al., 1986, p. 121). When low, capacity utilization enhances management's struggle to discipline labor by reducing investments and precipitating lower levels of production and higher levels of unemployment. At such times, management is in a better bargaining position and labor is forced to defend itself collectively. It is hypothesized that workers will strike in a defensive manner in response to management aggressions at those times when workers have some degree of institutional strength, but are economically vulnerable. In contrast, workers will strike in an aggressive manner as economic conditions recover, as capacity utilization improves, and as workers' relative power expands. Therefore, capacity utilization at the two digit industrial level, CAP, should be greater for aggressive strikes than for defensive ones during the month of the strike. CAP will be used in the discriminant analysis on the expectation that the lower it is, the more likely a given strike will be classified as defensive.

Injury Rate

Peter Arno (1982) has shown that injury rates tend to increase during business expansions and decline during recessionary phases of the business cycle. As Arno demonstrates, it is in the context of declining profitability during peak years of a business cycle that management strategy shifts towards an intensification of the labor process, pushing workers harder and de-emphasizing workplace safety. During such periods of relatively low unemployment, labor is in a position to fight back and encroach upon management's accustomed prerogatives by conducting aggressive strikes over working conditions. Therefore, it is hypothesized that increases in the injury rate (INJ) will increase the likelihood that a given strike will be aggressive.

Unfair Labor Practices

I have hypothesized earlier that management will be most aggressive, precipitating in unfair labor charges, during negotiations when labor is relatively weak. It is at such times that management attacks labor's previous gains. Consequently, as unfair labor practices as a percentage of production workers (UF) escalate, labor finds itself increasingly in a defensive posture. UF should provide a discriminant basis for dividing strikes—with a high level of unfair labor practices associated with defensive strikes and a low level with aggressive strikes.

Workers' Strength

Union Solidarity

It is hypothesized that job segregation by race and sex, whether initiated by the union or management, creates competitive tension among workers in a union and weakens its ability to conduct both defensive and aggressive strikes. Racial and sexual cohesion is vitally important for workers effectively to conduct both types of strikes. It is also hypothesized that, on average, defensive strikes will exhibit a *greater* degree of unity and solidarity. In contrast to offensive strikes, defensive strikes occur when workers have little economic leverage, when their ability to outlast employers' resistance is more dependent on their institutional strength. Calculations of success for defensive strike rely heavily on the union's ability to maintain racial stability and union cohesiveness. Offensive strikes, on the contrary, are timed when management has more to lose economically and when workers have less risk of unemployment. Calculations of success in such a situation, I would suggest, don't depend so heavily on union organizational strength and solidarity.

Therefore, I use indicators of union racial and gender inequality, UM, the ratio of male wages to female wages for unionized workers, and UB, the ratio of white wages to black wages for unionized workers, to discriminate between defensive and aggressive strikes on the expectation that low levels of racial inequality will identify those strikes that are defensive. For similar reasons I expect defensive strikes to be correlated with higher levels of union institutional strength. Union solidarity at every level is necessary for both types of strikes, aggressive and defensive. Nevertheless, to the extent that there is a difference between them, defensive strikes should exhibit greater solidarity because of the higher risks of failure. I will, therefore, use a proxy of union strength, the unionization rate in the state or region in which the strike occurs (SU), as a discriminating variable to distinguish between defensive and aggressive non-wage strikes.

Quits

Quits as a percentage of layoffs reflect workers' willingness and ability to struggle for better conditions and, therefore, should be relatively low when workers are not in a favorable economic climate to act independently. It is during such economic times that workers act defensively to protect previous gains that are under attack by management. Consequently, I will discriminate between aggressive and defensive strikes on the expectation that QL is significantly higher on average for aggressive strikes than defensive ones.

Economic Context of Class Relations

On the basis of the theoretical analysis outlined in chapter 4, I will include in the discriminant analysis a number of variables that reflect the economic costs imposed on management and labor during a strike.

I will also include the dummy variable, BC, to control for the effects of costs associated with the business cycle that are not already captured in the model. The logic of the model predicts that the economic costs facing management are greater during a strike in an upswing than a downswing, while the costs facing labor are greater during strike in a downswing than upswing. Accordingly, I hypothesize that defensive strikes are more likely to occur during a downswing, when management has relatively less to loose and labor has relatively more, and offensive strikes to occur during an upswing, when labor has relatively less to lose and management has relatively more. Therefore, I will use BC in the discriminant analysis on the expectation that an upswing will predict a strike to be offensive and a downswing will predict a strike to be defensive.

Management Vulnerability

As suggested earlier, the costs felt by management during a strike depend to a large degree on their ability to retain market shares. Management's ability to do so is expected to vary inversely with the percentage change in new orders in the month preceding the strike. In this case, employers forfeit the opportunity to add new customers in order to maintain or increase their market share during a strike. Therefore, I will use the percentage change in new orders the year preceding negotiations, PN, to discriminate between offensive and defensive strikes, hypothesizing that it is, on average, larger for offensive strikes than defensive ones.

Labor's Vulnerability

The principal cost to labor during a strike is referred to in this analysis as the cost of job loss. As already indicated, workers' resources fall as the percentage change in the cost of job loss the year preceding the strike increases: workers face longer unemployment duration and larger losses in income. Therefore, CJL, will be used to discriminate between aggressive and defensive strikes on the expectation that large values of CJL should act as good predictors of defensive strikes while smaller values should predict offensive strikes.

Summary

Combining all these variable definitions and functional specifications, a final specification for the discriminant function is arrived at for empirical estimation, using strike cases (m) that are known to fall either into a defensive or aggressive group (k).

$$D = B_0 + B_1CAP_{km} + B_2INJ_{km} + B_3UF_{km} + B_4UM_{km} + B_5UW_{km} + B_6SU_{km} + B_7QL_{km} + B_8PN_{km} + B_9CJL_{km} + B_{10}BC_{km} + B_{11}U_t$$

CAP	=	Percentage change in capacity utilization in firm's two digit industry for the year preceding the strike.
INJ	=	Two digit industrial injury rate for the year of strike.
UF	=	Ratio of unfair labor practices (section 8, NLRB) to number of production workers in firm's two digit industry for the strike year.
UM	=	Ratio of male wage to female wage rate for unionized workers in firm's two digit industry.
UW	=	Ratio of white wage to black wage rate for unionized workers in firm's two digit industry.
SU	=	Percent of all workers in state or region who are unionized.
QL	=	Ratio of quits to layoffs for 3 digit industry for the year of the strike.
PN	=	Percent change in new orders over the preceding year in the firm's 3 digit industry.
CJL	=	Percentage change in the cost of job loss in the firm's two digit industry for the twelve months preceding the strike.
BC	=	Dummy variable for business cycle based on the unemployment rate:
0	=	Upswing
1	=	Downswing

On the basis of the preceding discussion, it is hypothesized that the variables CAP, INJ, UF, UM, UB, QL, and PN are, on average, greater for offensive strikes than defensive strikes and SU, PC, and BC are greater for defensive strikes than offensive ones. Using these variables, the discriminant function is, in turn, hypothesized to be an effective method for differentiating between defensive and aggressive strikes.

2. Discriminant Results

The data set used for the following discriminant analysis, provided by the BLS, documents every strike in the 1970s that includes three or more workers. These data allow me to classify 110 strikes by their major issue and another 8,000 with the discriminant procedure (see the appendix for full details of the data).

A number of tests and statistics indicate the power of the discriminant function and the discriminating variables. One way of judging the substantive utility of a discriminant function is to examine the means of the discriminant scores for defensive and aggressive strikes. A test of the null hypothesis that in the populations from which the samples are drawn there is no difference between group means can be based on Wilks' Lambda. Wilks' Lambda is the ratio of the within-groups sum of squares to the total sum of squares. A lambda of 1 occurs when the mean of the discriminant scores are the same in all groups and there is no between groups variability. Values close to 0 occur when within-groups variability is small compares to the total variability—that is, when most of the total variability is attributable to differences between the means of the groups (Norusis, 1988, p. 5).

Table 2 shows that Wilks' Lambda is .53 and the observed significance level is .0019. On the basis of the significance level, the null hypothesis is rejected: it is highly unlikely that defensive strikes and offensive strikes have the same means on the discriminant scores and, therefore, it is safe to conclude provisionally that defensive and aggressive strikes, as theoretically defined, are not the same forms of working class militance.[6]

Even though Wilks' Lambda is statistically significant, it provides little information about the effectiveness of the function in classifying defensive and aggressive strikes. Small differences that are statistically robust do not always permit good discrimination among the two groups. The best guide to the predictive power of the function is the percentage of correct classifications. Once estimated, the discriminant scores are assigned to a group for which they have the largest probability of belonging.

Table 2.
Discriminant Analysis: Canonical Discriminant Function

Wilks Lambda	Significance
0.532	0.0019

Table 2.1.
Discriminant Analysis: Classification Results

Strike	No. of Cases	Predicted Strike	
		Defensive	Aggressive
Defensive	61	51	10
	(84%)	(16%)	
Aggressive	47	07	40
	(15%)	(85%)	
Ungrouped	8863	4176	4687
	(47%)	(53%)	

Percent of Strikes Correctly Classified: 84.3% (TAU = .74)

For cases used in the computation of the discriminant scores, actual group membership is known and can be compared to the predicted group. Table 2.1 shows that 84.3% of all strikes were correctly identified, including 84% of all defensive strikes (52 out of 61) and 85% of all aggressive strikes (40 out of 47). This classification rate easily outperforms the classification rate of 50% that is associated with pure random assignment. Another statistic in Table 2.1, tau, confirms this conclusion. Tau gives a standardized measure of improvement over random assignment.[7] The maximum value of tau is 1.0 and it occurs when there are no errors in prediction. A value of zero indicates no improvement. In this case, a tau of .74 means that the classification of strikes based on the discriminating variables made 74% fewer errors than would be expected by chance alone. These results indicate that the discriminant function effectively classifies strikes as either aggressive or defensive. This, in turn, indirectly confirms previous empirical work suggesting that defensive and aggressive strikes are distinct.

There are a number of ways to assess the contribution of a variable to the discriminant function. It is important in each case to gauge the power of a variable to discriminate between aggressive and defensive strikes. A preliminary measure of this power is a simple test for the univariate equality of group means for each variable. Table 2.2 shows the F value and its significance when each observation on every variable is divided either into a defensive or aggressive group. Only three of the key variables, PN, SU, and UF do not exhibit significant differences in group means. The hypothesis that the group means are equal is rejected for the rest of the variables at least the 5 percent level of significance. This means that the probability is less than .05 that the observed difference in sample means occurred by chance for these variables. These results buttress the contention that defensive strikes and aggressive strikes occur under different conditions and provide preliminary evidence that the discriminating variables are an effective basis for dividing strikes.

Table 2.2.
Discriminant Analysis: Univariate F-Ratio (106 degrees of freedom)

Variable	F	Significance
CAP	9.726	0.0023
INJ	4.367	0.0390
UF	2.395	0.1247
UM	6.717	0.0109
UW	11.47	0.0010
SU	0.9E-01	0.7627
QL	6.573	0.0118
PN	0.15E-01	0.9010
CJL	9.046	0.0033
BC	4.160	0.0439

A more thorough statistic, known as the "structure coefficient," examines the correlations between the values of the discriminant function and the values of the variables. The computation of the coefficients is straightforward: for each case the value of the discriminant function is computed, and the Pearson correlation coefficients between it and the original variables are obtained. Table 2.3 gives the pooled within-group correlations between discriminating variables and the values of the canonical discriminant function. The variables are ordered by size. This table also shows that the mean value for defensive strikes (group centroid) is -0.81, while the value for aggressive strikes is 1.05. This means that a negative sign on the correlation coefficient indicates that large variable values are associated with defensive strikes. Positive signs on the correlation coefficient, conversely, are associated with aggressive strikes.

The signs of the coefficients in Table 2.3 confirm the theoretical expectations of the model, with the exception that the sign on SU is reversed. Additionally, as prefigured by the univariate F-ratio, SU, PN and FU, are insignificantly correlated to the discriminant scores, adding little to the power of the discriminant function. These results suggests that these three variables have the same impact on labor's execution of an aggressive strike as they do on its execution of a defensive one.

SU, as a measure of a state's unionization rate, acts as a proxy for a community's solidarity with the union—in a more unionized region, greater ideological bonds with the union and more community cohesiveness should make it harder for management to attract 'scabs'. Therefore, it is likely that there will be more defensive and aggressive strikes in states with high unionization rates. Since defensive strikes and aggressive strikes mostly originate in the same states and regions, it is not surprising to find that state unionization rates do not contribute to the categorization of strikes as defensive or aggressive. Indeed, as Table 2.3 shows, SU, of all discriminating variables, has the lowest correlation with the discriminant scores.

Table 2.3.

Discriminant Analysis: Correlations between Discriminating Variables and Canonical Discriminant Function

Variable	Pearson Coefficient
UW	0.351 ***
CAP	0.323 ***
CJL	(0.312) ***
UM	0.269 ***
QL	0.266 ***
INJ	0.216 *
BC	(0.212) *
UF	0.161
PN	0.012
SU	0.006

Canonical Discriminant Function Group Centroids:

Aggressive Strikes: 1.06
Defensive Strikes: -0.82

*** = sig. at 1%; ** = sig. at 5%; * = sig. at 10% (two-tailed test)

On second thought, the weak correlation between unfair labor practices, UF, and the discriminant function scores may reflect management aggression when labor is at its weakest, unable to respond defensively and in no position to strike aggressively. When they are weak, unions, as a last resort, will turn to the formal filing of an unfair labor charge—an option that, on average, takes over 365 days to run its course and whose remedies are often viewed as inadequate to enforce national labor policy.[8] In this case, a large number of unfair labor practices may reflect labor's weakness and its inability to engage in any strike. Therefore, there might be little difference in the number of unfair labor practices surrounding defensive and aggressive strikes.[9]

Contrary to expectations, PN is also weakly correlated with the discriminant function. This may suggest that workers give little weight to PN in their decision to strike. Cynthia Gramm (1986) has suggested that this may be the case because unions are less privy than employers to information about early indicators in changes in demand for the product, rendering unions less likely to use PN as a gauge of the potential costs imposed on management during a strike. As such, it would be likely to show little difference between defensive and aggressive strikes.

The signs of the remaining seven coefficients are as expected and significant. Indicators for union discrimination show that racial and gender equality are essential for defensive strikes, confirming the assumption that workers must rely heavily on internal cohesion and solidarity during times when they are forced to defend themselves. During such times, as shown by CJL, workers are economically vulnerable, facing relatively high costs if they lose their jobs. In comparison, when the percent change in the cost of job loss is low, unions are more economically able to strike—and they do so aggressively, even those unions that are relatively more discriminatory against blacks and women. The coefficient on QL reflects workers' relative inability and unwillingness to quit when they are forced to strike defensively, compared to those times when they strike aggressively. Finally, CAP confirms that management's greatest power exists during recessionary times, allowing it to attack labor's prerogatives and forcing workers to collectively defend themselves.

Summary

The discriminant analysis proves to be a robust procedure for categorizing wage strikes as either defensive or aggressive. This sets the stage for a more thorough analysis that separately analyses the conditions surrounding all defensive and all aggressive strikes. To this end, the discriminant procedure provides strong, preliminary evidence for the ability of the model to distinguish between aggressive and defensive strikes according to the relative power of labor and capital. It also confirms expectations that defensive strikes occur when labor is economically vulnerable to management aggression; aggressive strikes, in contrast, occur when labor is in a better position to exact costs on management.

According to the discriminant classification, 53% of all strikes during the 1970s were aggressive while 47% were defensive. Figure

5 confirms that the timing of these strikes was very sensitive to the business cycle. Aggressive strikes escalated and defensive strikes fell during the economic expansion ending in 1973; and the onslaught of the 1974-75 recession predictably occasioned an increase in defensive strikes and a decrease in aggressive strikes. This same cycle repeated itself in the late 1970s, when the economy experienced an expansion until 1980. Here again, changes in the relative power of labor and management help explain the fluctuations in defensive and aggressive strike activity.

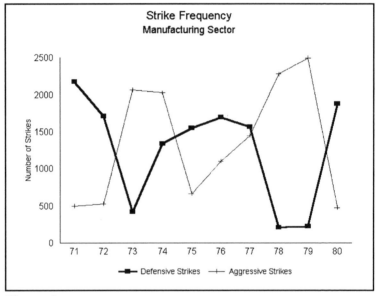

Figure 5.

NOTES

1. The strike data are from the BLS, "Historical Work Stoppages, United States, 1953-1981" on magnetic tape. A summary can be found in their annual publication, *Handbook of Labor Statistics*.

2. The BNA reports that the limitations on management's right to control production do not prevent management from making decision about physical shop conditions, like temperature and new machinery. Instead, limitations have the purpose of preventing speedups, excessive workloads and worker displacement that might result from changes in the production process. In many cases, contracts simply require management to notify the union prior to making substantial changes in operations (BNA, *Collective Bargaining Negotiations and Contracts, Basic Patterns*, 1987).

3. Most contracts specify the following as grounds for discharge or disciplinary action: violation of leave, unauthorized strike participation, unauthorized absence, dishonesty or theft, violation of company rules, intoxication, insubordination, incompetence or failure to meet standards, failure to obey safety rules, misconduct and tardiness (BNA, 1987).

4. Naples (1987) defines defensive strikes as work stoppages over job security and work load. According to the BLS ("Work Stoppages Historical File, 1952-1981"), job security includes seniority, discharge for age, alleged inefficiency, insubordination, indiscriminate discharges, layoffs and rehires, transfers, bumping and demotions, division of work, new machinery, supervisors doing production work, and excuses for absences. While all of my defensive non-wage strikes fall into Naples' list of defensive strikes, I have not included all of her defensive strike issues—it isn't always clear within the framework of the capital-labor accord whether some of these issues represent labor's initiative to provide better working conditions or labor's attempts to defend past gains. For this reason, I have left out alleged inefficiency, insubordination, transfers, transferring operations, division of work, new machinery, supervisors doing production work and excuses for absences from my list of defensive non wage strike issues.

5. The AIF was first adopted in the 1948 GM-UAW contract and was based on national productivity increases, which were then 3%.

6. Interpretations of the test of significance for the Wilks' Lambda should be conservative since there is no guarantee that the sample of strikes is independent and random. The benchmark for selecting this case is data availability. However, since the sample is relatively large (n=108) the test is still relevant.

7.

$$\tau = \frac{n_c - \sum_{i=1}^{g} p_i n_i}{n - \sum_{i=1}^{g} p_n n_i}$$

where nc is the number of cases correctly classified and pi is the prior probability of group membership

8. The NLRB has no independent statutory power of enforcement. It must seek enforcement in the U.S. Court of Appeals, and herein lies what management usually calls the "power of due process" and what unions call "premeditated attempts at continued delay" (Kovach, 1992). An employer found guilty of an unfair labor practice may appeal to a Court of Appeals where the time involved in processing the appeal can take years. Kovach (1982) cites the case of J.P. Stevens Co. where the company's persistent violations were in litigation for over ten years. The company chose to incur the minor punitive damages of the court and lawyer fees rather than to deal with its workers and their union.

9. This interpretation is supported by Byrne and King in the only strike study to consider unfair labor practices (1986). They conclude that wildcat strikes and complaints filed with the NLRB are "substitutes rather than complements." That is, the process of filing an unfair labor charge reduces the likelihood of unsanctioned strikes. They provide no strong theoretical reason for this result; yet, it is consistent with the interpretation that unfair labor charges reflect labor's inability to strike.

CHAPTER VI

Aggressive and Defensive Strike Propensity

A. Hypothesis

In this chapter, I test the relationship between the incidence of aggressive and defensive strikes and the power variables outlined in chapter IV. These tests will be conducted with separate probit analyses of defensive and aggressive strike propensity for 1,000 collective bargaining situations during 1971-1980.

To date, Cynthia Gramm (1986) provides the best and most detailed study of strike activity. Importantly, she acknowledges the need to model union and employer behavior. However, the greatest weakness of her analysis remains theoretical since she provides relatively little justification for the eclectic array of independent variables included in her analysis. As stated earlier, her inattention to many important additional dimensions of determination could also bias her results because of underspecifications. In order to address these weaknesses, I incorporate most of her variables into a larger, more theoretically anchored model. I assume that the probability of a strike occurring during contract negotiation i is given by the probit function:

$$Pr_i = 1 - P(B_0 + B_1UN_i + B_2INJ_i + B_3UF_i + B_4UM_i + B_5UW_i + B_6PM_i$$
$$+ B_7PW_i + B_8QL_i + B_9PN_i + B_{10}CJL_i + B_{11}BC_i + B_{12}EX_i + B_{13}SH_i +$$
$$B_{14}BC_i + B_{15}NO_i + B_{16}LC_i + B_{17}NS_i + B_{18}C_i + B_{19}INT_i + B_{20}HC_i + B_{21}SU_i$$
$$+ B_{22}U_i)$$

where $P(X)$ is the cumulative normal distribution and where the variables are defined in Appendix A. I include those variables from Gramm's probit estimation that are theoretically and statistically relevant to my analysis.

In order to avoid the problems inherent in a misspecified model and to capture the more complex dynamics of strike determination, I separately analyze aggressive and defensive strikes.

Aggressive Strikes. Aggressive strikes occur when labor's economic power is strengthened, *ceteris paribus*. If labor is institutionally strong and cohesive in such cases, then the likelihood that labor will strike over new demands will increase. For this reason, I expect the following signs for the effects of determinants of strike activity in a probit analysis of aggressive strikes: UN, UF, UW, UM, EX, CJL, BC, C, INT < 0; INJ, SU, PM, PW, QL, SH, PN, NO, LC, NS, HC > 0. Table 3 summarizes my expectations for aggressive strikes.

Defensive Strikes. The likelihood of a defensive strike increases as management's strength expands and management opportunistically attacks labor's previously won privileges. However, these strikes will only happen if labor is institutionally strong enough to respond with a strike. For these general reasons, I have the following sign expectations for a probit estimation of the direction of the determinants of defensive strike incidence, as summarized in Table 4: UW, UM, QL, EX, SH, PN, NO, C < 0; UF, UN, INJ, SU, PM, PW, CJL, BC > 0; and LC, NS, INT, HC = ?.

Table 3.
Determinants of Strike Activity

Aggressive Strikes

Variable	Sign Expectation

Capitalist Power

1.	State Unemployment Rate (UN)	-
2.	Injury Rate (INJ)	+
3.	Unfair Labor Practices (UF)	-

Workers' Strength

1.	State or Regional Unionization Rate (SU)	+
2.	Proportion of Male Union Workers (PM)	+
3.	Proportion of White Union Workers (PW)	+
4.	Relative Wage of White/Black Union Workers (UW)	-
5.	Relative Wage of Male/Female Union Workers (UM)	-
6.	Ratio of Quits to Layoffs (QL)	+

Workers' Expectations

1.	Ratio of Percent Change in Nominal Wage to Percent Change in CPI in Previous Contract (EX)	-

Capitalist Economic Vulnerability

1.	Coefficient of Variation in Shipments (SH)	+
2.	Annual Percentage Change in New Orders (PN)	+
3.	Percent of Previous Years New Orders Received the Quarter before Negotiations (NO)	+
4.	Ratio of Labor Costs to Value Added (LC)	+
5.	Proportion of Industry Workers who are Non-Supervisory (NS)	+

Workers' Economic Vulnerability

1.	Annual Percentage Change in the Cost of Job Loss (CJL)	-

Controls

1.	Business Cycle (BC)	-
2.	Wage-Price Controls (C)	-
3.	Interaction (INT)	-
4.	8 Firm Concentration Ratio (HC)	+

Table 4.
Determinants of Strike Activity

<u>Defensive Strikes</u>

<u>Variable</u>	<u>Sign Expectation</u>
Capitalist Power	
1. State Unemployment Rate (UN)	+
2. Injury Rate (INJ)	+
3. Unfair Labor Practices (UF)	+
Workers' Strength	
1. State or Regional Unionization Rate (SU)	+
2. Proportion of Male Union Workers (PM)	+
3. Proportion of White Union Workers (PW)	+
4. Relative Wage of White/Black Union Workers (UW)	-
5. Relative Wage of Male/Female Union Workers (UM)	-
6. Ratio of Quits to Layoffs (QL)	-
Workers' Expectations	
1. Ratio of Percent Change in Nominal Wage to Percent Change in CPI in Previous Contract (EX)	-
Capitalist Economic Vulnerability	
1. Coefficient of Variation in Shipments (SH)	-
2. Annual Percentage Change in New Orders (PN)	-
3. Percent of Previous Years New Orders Received the Quarter before Negotiations (NO)	-
4. Ratio of Labor Costs to Value Added (LC)	?
5. Proportion of Industry Workers who are Non-Supervisory (NS)	?
Workers' Economic Vulnerability	
1. Annual Percentage Change in Cost of Job Loss (CJL)	+
Controls	
1. Business Cycle (BC)	+
2. Wage-Price Controls (C)	-
3. Interaction (INT)	?
4. 8 Firm Concentration Ratio (HC)	?

B. Empirical Results

The data set used for the following probit estimations is derived from a single comprehensive sample of 6,046 contract negotiations occurring in 1971-1980 in bargaining units of 1,000 or more workers. This data, generously provided by Cynthia Gramm, provides 868 manufacturing collective bargaining negotiations with 62 defensive strikes and 58 aggressive strikes (see the appendix for full details of the data).

For the purposes of comparison, the first column in Table 5 reproduces results for all strikes of a probit estimate that only includes Gramm's explanatory variables. Column 5.2 provides my full model of explanatory variables and column 5.3 gives results of a stepwise elimination of the insignificant variables in column 5.2.

In column 5.1, I have left out three of Gramm's original variables because of severe multicollinearity: the ratio of outstanding consumer credit to disposable income, the effective prime interest rate on short term business loans during the month preceding the negotiation and a dummy variable indicating that the state in which the unit is located is a right to work state. These three variables have a correlation coefficient greater than .6 with key variables from my own model and their exclusion has no effect on the sign and significance of the other variables in Gramm's original presentation. I have also excluded two other variables that are consistently insignificant: the average number of dependent children of unionized workers in the industry and the percent of unionized workers in the industry who are married. Additionally, I find no strong theoretical reasons to include these later two variables.[1]

The results of the coefficient estimates in Table 5 should be interpreted with caution since the dependent variable measures the incidence of all strikes. By not dividing aggressive strikes from defensive ones, this approach masks underlying dynamics, once again biasing the results because of a misspecification. Nevertheless, by themselves, these results demonstrate the instability of Gramm's model: the full model changes the significance level of six of her original variables, including a shift of the unemployment rate into significance. Lacking any strong theoretical basis for including or eliminating

Table 5
Probit Coefficients for the Determinants
of the Probability of a Strike

		Gramm's Model 5.1	Full Model 5.2	5.3
C	Constant	-4.40 *** (1.48)	1.70 (2.69)	5.60 *** (1.88)
Capitalist Strength				
UN	State Unemployment Rate	0.04 (0.03)	0.10 ** (0.04)	0.09 *** (0.03)
INJ	Injury Rate	-	-0.17 (0.24)	-
INJ1	Injury Rate (t-1 year)	-	0.20 (0.27)	-
UF	Unfair Labor Practices	-	-1.00 ** (0.52)	-0.60 ** (0.31)
Workers' Strength				
PU	State Unionization Rate	0.03 *** (0.09)	0.02 ** (0.01)	-
PM	% Male	0.78 ** (0.32)	0.97 ** (0.46)	0.73 ** (0.40)
PW	% White	-1.20 (1.07)	-0.23 (1.19)	-
UM	Male Wages/Female Wages	-	-2.40 ** (1.20)	-3.04 *** (0.94)
UW	White Wages/Black Wages	-	-2.20 ** (1.10)	-3.57 *** (1.19)
QL	Quits/Layoffs	-	0.03 (0.05)	-
Workers' Expectations				
EX	% Wage/% CPI	-0.09 * (0.07)	-0.66 ** (0.48)	-0.14 ** (0.07)
Capitalist Economic Vulnerability				
SH	Variation in Shipments	-2.50 (2.16)	-3.66 * (2.48)	-
NO	New Orders (t-1 month)	0.08 ** (0.03)	0.05 * (0.04)	-
PN	New Orders (t-12 months)	-0.01 ** (0.004)	-0.01 ** (0.005)	-0.01 ** (0.003)
LC	Labor Costs/Value Added	2.21 (2.62) **	2.36 ** (1.02)	2.14 *** (0.89)
NS	% Non-Supervisory	-0.01 (0.006)	0.00 (0.008)	-
Workers' Economic Vulnerability				
CJL	Cost of Job Loss		-1.50 * (1.06)	-1.57 ** (0.89)

Table 5

(Cont'd)

		Gramm's Model	Full Model	
Controls				
BC	Business Cycle	-	0.49 (0.56)	-
C	Control	-	-0.30 ** (0.21)	-0.43 *** (0.16)
INT	Interaction (BC*UN)	-	-0.19 *** (0.07)	-0.12 *** (0.02)
INT	Interaction (BC*UN)	-	-0.19 *** (0.07)	-0.12 *** (0.02)
HC	Concencentration Ratio	0.33 *** (0.11)	0.24 ** (0.12)	0.24 ** (0.12)
	n	1108	926	1094
	Log Likelihood	-352	-314	-331
	Chi Squared	55.9 ***	86.18 ***	95.59 ***

Notes for All Tables:
Numbers in Parentheses are asymptotic standard errors.
*** = sig. at 1%; ** = sig. at 5%; * = sig. at 1% (on one tailed tests)
- indicates excluded from equation.

exogenous variables, Gramm's model, on its own terms, is not statistically robust, apparently omitting the relevant and significant variables of the larger model.

Table 6, columns 6.2 and 6.3 report the probit estimates for aggressive strikes while columns 6.4 and 6.5 give estimates for defensive strikes. I repeat previous results in column 5.1 for ease of comparison. The division of strikes has paid off. Four variables that were insignificant in the full model of all strikes are now significant for both defensive and aggressive strikes (all four with opposite sign directions for aggressive and defensive strikes); two other variables that were insignificant for all strikes are now significant for at least one of the other types of strikes; and no variable that was significant for all strikes is now insignificant for both defensive and aggressive strikes. In twelve of twenty-three cases, a variable that was significant for all strikes was significant for one of the other two types of strike—with five of these improving their significance level after the split into defensive and aggressive strikes. In general, the improvement in statistical results from the all-strikes specification to the two-grouped specification suggests that the complex dynamics surrounding these two groups of strikes are different and that a complete understanding of strike activity should account for this difference.

In all three specifications the goodness of fit measure, the log likelihood ratio test, is significant at the 1 percent level of significance. This test and the F-statistic in regression analysis are conceptually identical (Aldrech and Nelson, 1984, p.89). Unfortunately, there is no statistic in probit or logit analysis that allows for a goodness of fit test in the spirit of an adjusted R^2 in regression analysis. Therefore, goodness of fit tests in probit analysis are restricted to a test of the joint hypothesis that all coefficients except the intercept are zero; it is not possible to determine the proportion of the dependent variable that is explained by the exogenous variables.

In the following section, I detail the results for each variable in the model.

Table 6
Aggressive and Defensive Strike Propensity

		All Strikes	Aggressive Strikes		Defensive Strikes	
		6.1	6.2	6.3	6.4	6.5
C	Constant	1.70 (2.69)	-3.26 (3.46)	-2.40 (1.92)	13.70 *** (5.19)	9.80 *** (3.8)
Capitalist Strength						
UN	State Unemployment Rate	0.10 ** (0.04)	0.03 (0.06)	-	0.09 ** (0.05)	0.10 *** (0.04)
INJ	Injury Rate	-0.17 (0.24)	0.45 * (0.32)	0.46 * (0.29)	-0.85 *** (0.34)	-0.56 *** (0.24)
INJ1	Injury Rate (t-1 year)	0.20 (0.27)	-0.32 * (0.73)	-0.45 * (0.30)	0.99 *** (0.37)	0.69 *** (0.27)
UF	Unfair Labor Practices	-1.00 ** (0.52)	-0.63 (0.73)	-	-2.31 ** (0.77)	-1.72 *** (0.55)
Workers' Strength						
PU	State Unionization Rate	0.02 ** (0.01)	0.05 *** (0.01)	0.04 *** (0.14)	-0.01 (0.01)	-
PM	% Male	0.97 ** (0.46)	1.88 *** (0.69)	1.56 *** (0.60)	0.32 (0.61)	0.72 * (0.53)
PW	% White	-0.23 (1.19)	-0.77 (1.56)	-	-0.70 (1.62)	-
UM	Male Wages/Female Wages	-2.40 ** (1.20)	-3.46 ** (1.64)	-2.20 ** (1.25)	-4.19 *** (1.68)	-3.30 *** (1.30)
UW	White Wages/Black Wages	-2.20 ** (1.10)	-0.33 (1.17)	-	-9.31 *** (2.78)	-8.56 *** (2.50)
QL	Quits/Layoffs	0.03 (0.05)	0.13 *** (0.05)	0.12 *** (0.05)	-0.15 ** (0.09)	-0.15 ** (0.07)
Workers' Expectations						
EX	% Wage/% CPI	-0.66 * (0.48)	-0.30 *** (0.10)	-0.24 *** (0.09)	0.0 (0.0)	
Capitalist Economic Vulnerability						
SH	Variation in Shipments	-3.66 * (2.48)	1.38 (3.16)	-	-10.1 *** (3.63)	-7.03 *** (2.90)
NO	New Orders (t-1 month)	0.05 * (0.04)	0.02 (0.05)	-	0.10 ** (0.05)	0.09 ** (0.04)
PN	New Orders (t-12 months)	-0.01 ** (0.005)	-0.02 *** (0.007)	-0.01 ** (0.005)	-0.00 (0.001)	-
LC	Labor Costs/Value Added	2.36 ** (1.02)	2.69 ** (1.30)	2.36 ** (1.14)	0.29 (1.47)	-
NS	% Non-Supervisory	0.00 (0.008)	0.02 * (0.013)	0.01 * (0.01)	0.00 (0.01)	-
Workers' Economic Vulnerability						
CJL	Cost of Job Loss	-1.50 * (1.06)	-3.34 *** (1.40)	-3.28 *** (1.14)	1.46 (1.44)	1.57 * (1.23)

Table 6
(cont'd)

		All Strikes	Aggressive Strikes		Defensive Strikes	
		6.1	6.2	6.3	6.4	6.5
Controls						
BC	Business Cycle	0.49 (0.56)	-1.20 ** (0.89)	-1.11 *** (0.38)	1.02 * (0.65)	0.87 ** (0.54)
C	Control	-0.30 ** (0.21)	-0.76 ** (0.36)	0.66 ** (0.33)	-0.05 (0.25)	-
INT	Interaction (BC*UN)	-0.19 *** (0.07)	-0.06 (0.12)	-	-0.25 *** (0.08)	-0.19 *** (0.07)
HC	Concentration Ratio	0.24 ** (0.12)	0.45 *** (0.16)	0.45 *** (0.15)	-0.04 (0.17)	-
	n	926	926	927	927	926
	Log Likelihood	-314	-179	-187	-177	-214
	Chi Squared	86.14 ***	95.22 ***	81.95 ***	78.48 ***	76.65 ***

The Business Cycle.

Once all strikes are divided in Table 6, the control for the business cycle, BC, becomes significant and has the expected opposite signs for defensive and aggressive strikes. This indicates that these strike occur at very different times in the business cycle, when both labor and management face very different economic conditions. The different timing of these strikes is further reinforced by the probit results on the interaction term between the business cycle and the state unemployment rate, INT. For aggressive strikes, INT is insignificant and doesn't add to the model. However, for defensive strikes, it is significant and negative. Along with the results on BC, this indicates that even though defensive strikes occur during a downswing, the likelihood of a defensive strike decreases as unemployment increases and the economy deteriorates during the downswing. This supports the contention that defensive strikes are directly related to a souring economy but that continuing increases in unemployment render workers increasingly vulnerable to labor market competition and therefore less and less willing to engage in defensive strikes. Therefore, aggressive strikes occur during the upswing and defensive strikes seem to develop in the early stages of the downswing when the economy first experiences a slowdown and decrease as the economy worsens.

Management's Economic Vulnerability

Other economic conditions prove to have important influences on strike behavior, but not always as anticipated. In particular, the results of three indicators of management's economic vulnerability, SH, PN and NO, are at least provocative, if not always expected.

1. SH acts as a proxy for management's ability to maintain its market share during a strike; for defensive strikes, column 6.4 shows, as expected, that management pushes labor out on strike when its market share is less at risk. Unfortunately, the coefficient is consistently insignificant for aggressive strikes.

2. Contrary to expectations, PN, the percentage change in new orders over the preceding year in the unit's industry, is significant and negative for aggressive strikes. Although negative as expected, PN is

insignificant for defensive strikes. As suggested in the preceding chapter, these results may indicate that management gives greater weight to PN in their decision calculus than workers. As sales and new orders increase, management is in a better position to know this and perhaps more willing to accede to labor's demands. Labor, for its part, might not look to PN as a basis for escalating strikes. Instead of looking at long-term changes in product demand to time its strikes, labor might look at short-term seasonal changes as a way gauging the potential economic damage inflicted on management. Therefore, over the long run, as PN increases, I now surmise that aggressive strike activity falls because management is more receptive to labor's demand and less willing to provoke labor.

3. Equally unexpected is the positive and significant coefficient for NO on defensive strikes. NO indicates whether the contract expiration coincides with a season of high demand when the loss of customers due to a strike would be higher than in seasons of low demand. Certainly management may be more aggressive during stagnant economic times, but the results in columns 6.4 and 6.5 indicate that labor will defend itself during seasons of relatively high demand when it has a good chance of creating some economic costs for management.[2] Unfortunately, the coefficients for NO in columns 6.2 and 6.3 are insignificant, making the effects of NO on aggressive strikes inconclusive.

Expectations about the relationship between strike incidence and management's ability to maintain production are confirmed by the coefficients on LC and NS. Columns 6.2 and 6.3 provide support of the hypothesis that workers aggressively strike when management is less able to maintain production, either when labor costs represent a large proportion of an industry's value added (LC) or when the proportion of workers who are employed in non-supervisory production and service jobs is relatively large (NS).[3] Furthermore, the coefficients on LC and NS in column 6.4 are insignificant, supporting the contention, as anticipated, that they have a contradictory effect on defensive strike activity since, in this case, they simultaneously capture management's ability to maintain production and labor's institutional lack of numbers.

Workers' Economic Vulnerability

The cost of job loss provides additional evidence in support of the model. An indicator of the economic vulnerability of labor, the percentage change in the annual cost of job loss shows, as expected, that workers strike aggressively as their economic position improves and are forced to defend themselves as their economic position deteriorates. For aggressive strikes, the coefficients of CJL in columns 6.2 and 6.3 are significant at the 1 percent level and have their expected negative signs; for defensive strikes the coefficient is significant at the 10 percent level in column 6.5 and has the expected positive sign.

Workers' Expectations

Inflationary pressures seem to have a positive impact on aggressive strike activity, but not, as expected, on defensive strikes. Table 6 shows that EX is negative and significant at the 1 percent level for aggressive strikes and insignificant for defensive strikes. Aggressive strikes certainly seem to be positively influenced by the "catch-up" behavior generated by high levels of inflation. It seems, as expected, that workers expect to maintain the standard of living to which they have become accustomed, hence to catch up with prices by asking for unusually large wage gains if earnings have not kept pace with inflation over the term of the previous contract. In fact, these results suggests that "catch-up" wage strikes created by high inflation are aggressive, not defensive.

Not surprisingly, the Nixon wage-price controls, C, follow the same pattern as EX—they are negative and significant for aggressive strike and insignificant for defensive ones. This seems to confirm that unanticipated inflation creates "catch-up aggressive" strikes since the controls diminish the need to catch-up, decreasing aggressive strikes and leaving defensive strikes untouched.

Workers' Strength

Expectations about the importance of institutional cohesion and strength on the incidence of all types of strikes are provisionally supported. Table 6 shows that the coefficients on the indicators of racial and sexual inequality in the form of job segregation, UM and UW, are consistently negative and significant for all defensive strike estimations. UM is also significant and negative as expected for aggressive strikes. However, UW has an insignificant coefficient for aggressive strikes. This unanticipated result may suggest that racial inequality in job assignments is less divisive and debilitating than similar gender inequalities—a conclusion mirrored in the persistent positive significance of PM, a proxy for sexual prejudice, and the consistent insignificance of PW, a proxy for racial prejudice. However, these results should be interpreted with caution because these indicators, acting as imperfect measures of job segregation and prior prejudices, may be capturing other industry-specific effects. In fact, PW is correlated with HI, a dummy variable measuring the industry's eight-firm concentration ratio; and UW is correlated with the industry's ratio of labor costs to value added, LC.[4] In both cases, PW and UW are also serving as indicators of core manufacturing industries that have a high percentage of oligopolistic firms and have larger union movements. Although I control for these effects by including HI and LC in all the probit estimations, the equations may still understate the impact of racism because the proxies of racial inequality may be still picking up these and other dimensions of the core sector.

Another institutional determinant, the state unionization rate, is significant and has its expected sign in the probit estimation of aggressive strikes in Table 6. However, the lack of significance in the defensive equation is surprising. On the assumption that workers only protect themselves with defensive strikes when threatened, I estimated an alternative specification that incorporated an interaction effect between PU and QL. In this case, QL acts as an indicator of workers' greatest threat—layoffs. For this specification, defensive strikes should escalate only when workers' experience a relatively large number of layoffs in the those states that are unionized. Columns 7.3 and 7.4 in Table 7 present the interactive effect as the product of the unionization rate and the ratio of quits to layoffs. I repeat previous results for defensive strikes in columns 7.1 and 7.2 for ease of comparison. For reasons of completeness, I have also included the

Table 7
Alternative Specification
of Aggressive and Defensive Strike Propensity

		Defensive Strikes				Aggressive Strikes
		Original Specification		Alternate Specification		Alternate
		7.1	7.2	7.3	7.4	7.5
C	Constant	13.70 ***	9.80 ***	11.90 **	7.43 **	3.18 ***
		(5.19)	(3.8)	(5.26)	(3.67)	(3.8)
Capitalist Strength						
UN	State Unemployment Rate	0.09 **	0.10 ***	0.09 **	0.10 **	-
		(0.05)	(0.04)	(0.05)	(0.05)	
INJ	Injury Rate	-0.85 ***	-0.56 ***	-0.86 ***	-0.70 ***	0.46 **
		(0.34)	(0.24)	(0.34)	(0.23)	(0.36)
INJ1	Injury Rate (t-1 year)	0.99 ***	0.69 ***	1.00 ***	0.90 ***	-0.45 *
		(0.37)	(0.27)	(0.30)	(0.31)	(0.36)
UF	Unfair Labor Practices	-2.31 **	-1.72 ***	-2.36 ***	-1.62 **	-
		(0.77)	(0.55)	(0.79)	(0.55)	
Workers' Strength						
PU	State Unionization Rate	-0.01	-	0.03 *	0.03 *	0.07 ***
		(0.01)		(0.03)	(0.03)	(0.02)
PM	% Male	0.32	0.72 *	0.27	-	2.02 ***
		(0.61)	(0.53)	(0.61)		(0.71)
PW	% White	-0.70	-	-0.26	-	-
		(1.62)		(1.26)		
UM	Male Wages/Female Wages	-4.19 ***	-3.30 ***	-3.86 ***	-4.37 ***	-3.39 ***
		(1.68)	(1.30)	(1.19)	(1.19)	(1.44)
UW	White Wages/Black Wages	-9.31 ***	-8.56 ***	-9.36 ***	-6.29 ***	-
		(2.78)	(2.50)	(2.79)	(2.18)	
QL	Quits/Layoffs	-0.15 **	-0.15 **	0.39 **	0.28 *	0.39 **
		(0.09)	(0.07)	(0.25)	(0.20)	(0.20)
Workers' Expectations						
EX	% Wage/% CPI	0.0	-	0.03	-	-0.26 ***
		(0.09)		(0.09)		(0.10)
Capitalist Economic Vulnerability						
SH	Variation in Shipments	-10.1 ***	-7.03 ***	-9.99 ***	-8.3 ***	-
		(3.63)	(2.90)	(3.62)	(2.79)	
NO	New Orders (t-1 month)	0.10 **	0.09 **	0.11 **	0.10 **	-
		(0.05)	(0.04)	(0.05)	(0.04)	
PN	New Orders (t-12 months)	-0.00	-	-0.01	-	-0.02 **
		(0.001)		(0.01)		(0.007)
LC	Labor Costs/Value Added	0.29	-	0.12	-	3.06 **
		(1.47)		(1.54)		(1.30)
NS	% Non-Supervisory	0.00	-	-0.01	-	-
		(0.01)		(0.01)		
Workers' Economic Vulnerability						
CJL	Cost of Job Loss	1.46	1.57 *	1.52	1.99 **	-2.88 **
		(1.44)	(1.23)	(1.47)	(1.24)	(1.39)

Labor Strife and the Economy in the 1970s

Table 7
(cont'd)

		Defensive Strikes				Aggressive Strikes
		Original Specification		Alternate Specification		Alternate
		7.1	7.2	7.3	7.4	7.5
Controls						
BC	Business Cycle	1.02 * (0.65)	0.87 ** (0.54)	0.93 * (0.67)	0.76 * (0.54)	-
C	Control	-0.05 (0.25)	-	-0.10 (2.63)	-	-0.68 ** (0.35)
INT	Interaction (BC*UN)	-0.25 *** (0.08)	-0.19 *** (0.07)	-0.24 *** (.89)	-0.30 *** (0.13)	-
HC	Concentration Ratio	-0.04 (0.17)	-	-0.05 (0.15)	-	0.43 *** (0.16)
PQL	PU*QL	-	-	-0.24 ** (0.01)	-0.02 *** (0.01)	-0.01 (0.01)
	n	926	926	927	927	926
	Log Likelihood	-177	-214	-175	-211	177
	Chi Squared	78.5 ***	76.7 ***	82.0 ***	78.5 ***	76.7 ***

interactive effect in the best specification for aggressive strikes in column 7.5.

The coefficient of the state unionization rate is positive and significant for defensive strikes in this alternative formulation. In addition, the coefficient on the interaction term, PQL, is significant and negative in columns 7.3 and 7.4. These results indicate that increases in layoffs and the subsequent deceases in QL improve the likelihood of a defensive strike. In fact, the nature of the interaction effect is colinear in form, and for every one unit that QL changes, the coefficient on PU changes by the magnitude of the coefficient on the interactive term.[5] That is, the overall effect of PU on defensive strikes will be positive for any industry with QL less than one. Although QL turns positive in this formulation, once again, as expected, the interaction term demonstrates that QL has an overall negative relationship with defensive strikes in those states that are highly unionized: the effect of QL on defensive strikes will be negative for states with unionization rates greater than 14%. The defensive equation specified in column 7.4 represents a superior approach than the specification in Table 6: column 7.4 adds additional information without rendering other variables insignificant. Finally, Table 7, column 7.5, shows that PQL has an insignificant effect on aggressive strikes and, therefore, need not be considered for these strikes.

Returning to Table 6, QL, acting as a proxy for worker independence, has a positive relationship with aggressive strike incidence; QL has the expected positive sign and is significant at the 5 percent level. These results, along with those for defensive strikes, suggest that workers' collective action reflects their individual actions: those times when workers are able and willing to act independently coincide with those times that they collectively and aggressively strike for better work conditions; in contrast, those times when they are vulnerable, less able and willing to act independently coincide more with times when they are forced in highly unionized states to defend themselves and to strike against management attacks on established privileges.

Capitalist Strength

Unemployment

Additional results on the relationship between state unemployment rates and strike behavior provide support for the hypothesis that unemployment acts as a further indicator of shifts of relative power between capital and labor and sets the economic context for either antagonistic managerial behavior, precipitating defensive strikes, or aggressive workers' behavior, precipitating aggressive strikes. As anticipated, the coefficient on UN in column 6.4 shows that a high degree of unemployment, on average, has a positive influence on the incidence of defensive strikes—strikes that labor uses to defend itself against management encroachments. In addition, as already indicated, the coefficient on the interaction term, INT, illustrates the inhibiting influence of additional increases in unemployment on defensive strikes during business cycle downswings. Unfortunately, for aggressive strikes, the coefficients on the state unemployment rate (columns 6.2 and 6.3) consistently have the wrong sign and are insignificant.

Nonetheless, the inclusion of state unionization rates in the model allows for the test of an intriguing explanation for these results. It seems likely that low unemployment rates will have their largest impact on the incidence of aggressive strikes in those states that are highly unionized. In other words, the state unionization rate is likely to influence the impact of low unemployment on aggressive strike activity. In this case, the state unionization rate may be picking up on some of the effects of the state unemployment rate. In Table 8, I test this explanation with an alternative specification that includes an interaction term between the state unemployment rate and the state unionization rate. Table 8 follows the same presentation as earlier tables, with a comparison of previous results for aggressive strikes and the inclusion of the interactive effect in the best defensive strike specification.

The new aggressive strike equation proves to be a better specification of the model: UN is now negative and significant in columns 8.3 and 8.4, indicating that aggressive strikes occur as expected—when workers face a tight labor market. The positive and

Table 8
Another Alternative Specification of
Aggressive and Defensive Strike Propensity

| | | Aggressive Strikes | | | | Defensive Strikes |
| | | Original Specification | | Alternate Specification | | Alternate |
		8.1	8.2	8.3	8.4	8.5
C	Constant	-3.26 (3.46)	-2.40 (1.92)	0.27 (3.85)	3.77 (2.43)	14.10 (5.3)
Capitalist Strength						
UN	State Unemployment Rate	0.03 (0.06)	-	-0.45 ** (0.26)	-0.47 ** (0.26)	-
INJ	Injury Rate	0.45 * (0.32)	0.46 * (0.29)	0.51 ** (0.34)	0.52 ** (0.30)	-0.85 *** (0.36)
INJ1	Injury Rate (t-1 year)	-0.32 * (0.73)	-0.45 * (0.30)	-0.51 * (0.35)	-0.51 ** (0.31)	0.98 *** (0.36)
UF	Unfair Labor Practices	-0.63 (0.73)	-	0.04 (0.67)	-	-2.30 *** (0.70)
Workers' Strength						
PU	State Unionization Rate	0.05 *** (0.01)	0.04 *** (0.14)	-0.07 (0.06)	-	-
PM	% Male	1.88 *** (0.69)	1.56 *** (0.60)	1.64 *** (0.61)	1.64 *** (0.61)	-
PW	% White	-0.77 (1.56)	-	-0.68 (1.56)	-	-
UM	Male Wages/Female Wages	-3.46 ** (1.64)	-2.20 ** (1.25)	-3.70 *** (1.39)	-3.30 *** (1.19)	-4.18 *** (1.69)
UW	White Wages/Black Wages	-0.33 (1.17)	-	-0.25 (1.22)	-	-
QL	Quits/Layoffs	0.13 *** (0.05)	0.12 *** (0.05)	0.12 ** (0.05)	0.13 *** (0.05)	-0.15 ** (0.09)
Workers' Expectations						
EX	% Wage/% CPI	-0.30 *** (0.10)	-0.24 *** (0.09)	-0.26 *** (0.10)	-0.2 *** (0.09)	-
Capitalist Economic Vulnerability						
SH	Variation in Shipments	1.38 (3.16)	-	1.45 (3.15)	-	9.99 *** (3.63)
NO	New Orders (t-1 month)	0.02 (0.05)	-	0.02 (0.05)	-	0.10 ** (0.05)
PN	New Orders (t-12 months)	-0.02 *** (0.007)	-0.01 ** (0.005)	-0.01 *** (0.01)	-0.01 *** (0.00)	-
LC	Labor Costs/Value Added	2.69 ** (1.30)	2.36 ** (1.14)	3.01 ** (1.30)	2.72 *** (1.14)	-
NS	% Non-Supervisory	0.02 * (0.013)	0.01 * (0.01)	0.01 (0.02)	0.02 ** (0.01)	-
Workers' Economic Vulnerability						
CJL	Cost of Job Loss	-3.34 *** (1.40)	-3.28 *** (1.14)	-2.90 *** (1.36)	-3.60 *** (1.31)	-

Table 8
(cont'd)

		Aggressive Strikes				Defensive Strikes
		Original Specification		Alternate Specification		Alternate
		8.1	8.2	8.3	8.4	8.5

Controls

BC	Business Cycle	-1.20 ** (0.89)	-1.11 *** (0.38)	-0.96 ** (0.44)	-0.98 *** (0.38)	-
C	Control	-0.76 ** (0.36)	0.66 ** (0.33)	-0.67 ** (0.34)	-0.68 ** (0.33)	-
INT	Interaction (BC*UN)	-0.06 (0.12)	-	-	-	-0.26 *** (0.09)
HC	Concentration Ratio	0.45 *** (0.16)	0.45 *** (0.15)	0.42 *** (0.15)	0.47 *** (0.15)	-
PUN	PU*UN	-	-	0.02 ** (0.01)	0.02 ** (0.01)	0.00 (0.01)
	n	926	926	927	927	926
	Log Likelihood	-177	-186	-178	-180	177
	Chi Squared	95.2 ***	81.9 ***	98.4 ***	91.6 ***	112 ***

significant coefficient on the interaction term, PUN, shows, as expected, that unionization rates positively influence the impact of unemployment on aggressive strike activity. The coefficient on state unionization turns negative and insignificant in the alternative specification. Coupled with the positive interaction term, PUN, this result suggests that unionization is important to the conduct of aggressive strikes once unemployment has surpassed a certain level (3.5%). At lower levels of unemployment, state unionization contributes little to aggressive strikes; if the state unemployment rate moved to zero, the contribution of state unionization would not be significantly different from zero. Such low levels of unemployment create considerable economic leverage for workers in their struggle with management—so much so that regional solidarity and cohesiveness in the form of state unionization rates is not important. The ease with which workers can disrupt production and also find alternative employment is enough to engender aggressive strikes, irregardless of regional solidarity. The aggressive equation specified in column 8.4 represents a superior approach than the specification in Table 6: column 8.4 adds additional information without rendering other variables insignificant. Finally, the results of the new specification for defensive strikes show that these strikes do not exhibit the same dynamic as aggressive strikes: PUN is insignificant and UN is rendered insignificant in column 8.5.

Unfair Labor Practices

The results in Tables 6-8 on the variable UF, unfair labor practices filed against management in a given industry, corroborate the empirical conclusions of the discriminant analysis that management seems to disrupt collective bargaining procedures only when labor is at its weakest, when workers are in no position to respond with either an aggressive strike or a defensive one. All of the specifications show that UF has the expected negative sign for defensive strikes and is significant at least the 5 percent level. Surprisingly however, UF is insignificant for all aggressive strike specifications. A puzzling result, it may stem from the strong correlation of .46 between UF and PM, suggesting that the latter may be picking up some of the former's effects. However, an alternative specification that excludes PM does not affect the significance level of UF in any specification in Tables 6-8. This result may indicate that UF may be picking up on some other unspecified industry effects that render it insignificant.

Injury Rate

Peter Arno (1982) shows that the industrial injury rate soared in the 1970s as the capital-labor accord unraveled and a restructuring of the economy began to take place. In the context of a declining economy, declining profitability and a slowdown in productivity, management's strategy in the 1970s appears to have shifted toward an intensification of the labor process that pushed workers harder and de-emphasized workplace safety. As already indicated, the industrial injury rate pattern for the postwar period shows that a decline in the 1950s was followed by a dramatic increase during the unraveling of the accord in the late 1960s and 1970s. These increases undermined workers' commitment to industrial peace.

All of the specifications in Tables 6-8 show a consistent pattern: an escalation in the industrial injury rate increases the likelihood of defensive and aggressive strikes. The coefficients on the injury rate for the year of negotiations and the preceding year are significant for both defensive and aggressive strikes. In addition, the sum of these coefficients is consistently positive for both types of strikes, indicating that high injury rates over the two years before negotiations have, in total, a positive effect on strike incidence.

In order to assess the joint contribution of INJ and INJ1 on strike activity, I have included tests of the null hypothesis that the two coefficients are jointly equal to zero. The difference between the value of the -2*(log likelihood ratio) of a constrained model that excludes INJ and INJ1 and that of a unconstrained model that includes them can be evaluated using a chi-squared test with the degrees of freedom equal to the value obtained by subtracting the degrees of freedom of the constrained model from the degrees of freedom of the unconstrained model.[6] In every case, the resulting chi-squared statistic is significant at the 1% level of significance. Together, these two variables were consistently robust and added significantly to the model's explanation of defensive and aggressive strike propensity.

Control Variables

I include one other control variable that is often used in the literature, the 8-firm concentration ratio. The results in Tables 6-8 consistently show that the 8-firm concentration ratio is significant for aggressive strikes but not defensive ones. This provides modest support for the hypothesis that increases in the 8-firm concentration ratio are reflective of large, unionized workforces that are in a better position to act aggressively than workforces in industries that are less unionized (see Gordon, Edwards, Reich, 1982; Reich, 1979; and Oster, 1979).[7]

In conclusion, the specifications that best represent my approach are found in Table 7, column 7.4, for defensive strikes and Table 8, column 8.4, for aggressive strikes. In both cases, these specifications add interactive terms to the original specifications in Table 6, making the equations more dynamic and robust without sacrifice.

Statistical Considerations

The use of panel data calls into question some of the usual assumptions about the stochastic component of the model. This difficulty arises because the disturbance term might consist of time-series-related disturbances, cross-section disturbances, or a combination of both (Pindyck and Rubinfield, 1981, p. 252-261). In particular, omitted variables may lead to changing cross-section and time series intercepts. The model may fail to control for bargaining unit specific factors or time specific factors.

The inclusion of year dummy variables is designed to allow the intercept term to vary over time, correcting for contemporaneous correlation. The first year dummy variable is omitted since its addition would result in perfect collinearity between the constant term and the sum of the dummy variables. The problem of cross-sectional correlation, or serial correlation, cannot be corrected because the cross-sections vary in size—some variables are collected at the 3-digit industrial level, others at the 2-digit industrial level while others are collected at the state level. Although the probit coefficients are asymptotically unbiased in this case, their estimated variances are not, which suggests that caution should be used in interpreting the results of the hypothesis tests (Robinson, 1982).

The choice of whether to use year dummy variables is one that can be made on the basis of statistical testing. In regression analysis, an F statistic can be used to test the joint hypothesis that a subset of coefficients are zero. A corresponding test in probit analysis that serves the same purpose is based on the likelihood ratio principle outlined above. The subset of coefficients in this case includes all of the dummies. The resulting chi-squared test then allows for a goodness of fit test for the yearly dummies. Finally, t-tests on the coefficients provide an indication of the ability of the individual dummies to capture important missing information in the model.

Table 9 provides results of probit estimations with and without yearly dummy variables for aggressive and defensive strike estimations. I was forced to drop the dummies BC and C from the expanded model because there was perfect collinearity between each of these two variables and the year dummies. Despite the exclusion of BC and C, the coefficients on the individual year dummies for both aggressive and defensive strikes are not significantly different than zero. They fail in both cases to capture any uncontrolled secular trends. In addition, the chi-squared test doesn't reject the null hypothesis for both defensive and aggressive strikes. This means that the dummies, as a subset of variables, are not significantly different from zero. Together, these two results suggest that the year dummies are not robust enough to include in aggressive and defensive strike estimations. Indeed, this result suggests that the model adequately controls for time specific factors without dummy variables.

In regard to a separate issue, it can be argued that the results of the probit analysis of aggressive and defensive strike activity are prefigured by a discriminant analysis whose purpose is to identify the majority of strikes as aggressive or defensive. Unemployment, for instance, is used by the discriminant analysis to identify aggressive and defensive strikes, assigning strikes in states with relatively high unemployment rates as defensive, other things equal, and strikes with relatively low unemployment rates as aggressive. Unemployment is then used to analyze defensive strikes and aggressive strikes in separate probit analysis and, not surprisingly, as unemployment increases, defensive strikes increase and as unemployment decreases,

Table 9
Aggressive and Defensive Strike Propensity
(with Year Dummies, 1972-1980)

		Aggressive Strikes		Defensive Strikes	
		9.1	9.2	9.3	9.4
C	Constant	-2.40 (1.92)	-4.61 (3.45)	9.80 *** (3.8)	10.58 *** (4.00)
Capitalist Strength					
UN	State Unemployment Rate	-	-	0.10 *** (0.04)	0.05 ** (0.03)
INJ	Injury Rate	0.46 * (0.29)	0.26 (0.36)	-0.56 *** (0.24)	-0.72 *** (0.31)
INJ1	Injury Rate (t-1 year)	-0.45 * (0.30)	-0.29 (0.38)	0.69 *** (0.27)	0.87 *** (0.34)
UF	Unfair Labor Practices	-	-	-1.72 *** (0.55)	-1.59 *** (0.60)
Workers' Strength					
PU	State Unionization Rate	0.04 *** (0.14)	0.05 *** (0.14)	-	-
PM	% Male	1.56 *** (0.60)	1.76 *** (0.66)	0.72 * (0.53)	-
PW	% White	-	-	-	-
UM	Male Wages/Female Wages	-2.20 ** (1.25)	-2.20 ** (1.36)	-3.30 *** (1.30)	-3.60 *** (1.31)
UW	White Wages/Black Wages	-	-	-8.56 *** (2.50)	-9.40 *** (2.26)
QL	Quits/Layoffs	0.12 *** (0.05)	0.10 ** (0.05)	-0.15 ** (0.07)	-0.18 ** (0.08)
Workers' Expectations					
EX	% Wage/% CPI	-0.30 *** (0.10)	-0.17 ** (0.10)	-	-
Capitalist Economic Vulnerability					
SH	Variation in Shipments	-	-	-7.03 *** (2.90)	-7.61 *** (3.02)
NO	New Orders (t-1 month)	-	-	0.09 ** (0.04)	0.07 ** (0.04)
PN	New Orders (t-12 months)	-0.01 ** (0.005)	-0.01 ** (0.006)	-	-
LC	Labor Costs/Value Added	2.36 ** (1.14)	3.08 *** (1.22)	-	-
NS	% Non-Supervisory	0.01 * (0.01)	0.02 * (0.01)	-	-

Table 9
(cont'd)

		Aggressive Strikes		Defensive Strikes	
		9.1	9.2	9.3	9.4
Workers' Economic Vulnerability					
CJL	Cost of Job Loss	-3.28 *** (1.14)	-6.86 *** (2.80)	1.57 * (1.23)	-0.66 (2.61)
Controls					
BC	Business Cycle	-1.11 *** (0.38)	-	0.87 ** (0.54)	-
C	Control	0.66 ** (0.33)		-	-
INT	Interaction (BC*UN)	-	-	-0.19 *** (0.07)	0.02 (0.31)
HC	Concentration Ratio	0.45 *** (0.15)	0.43 *** (0.16)	-	-
YEAR	Two		0.32 (3.90)		-0.21 (2.41)
	Three		1.20 (2.88)		1.77 (1.87)
	Four		1.34 (2.85)		1.31 (1.49)
	Five		1.46 (2.81)		0.56 (1.55)
	Six		2.39 (2.80)		1.58 (1.78)
	Seven		1.29 (2.82)		1.67 (1.81)
	Eight		1.32 (2.87)		0.72 (1.91)
	Nine		1.42 (2.90)		-0.12 (2.00)
	Ten		-0.67 (2.99)		0.38 (1.57)
	n	927	927.00	926	926.00
	Log Likelihood	-187	-172.70	-214	-173.70
	Chi Squared	81.95 ***	79.90 ***	76.65 ***	76.65 ***
	Joint Test for Dummies		19.80		19.38

aggressive strikes increase. The question becomes: is my probit analysis self-fulfilling because of the discriminant results?

Statistically, the one factor that the discriminant analysis has predetermined is the difference in group means for the observations on each variable: the mean of the unemployment rate is statistically larger for defensive strike than aggressive strikes. However, the discriminant analysis does not prefigure the multivariate correlation between strike activity and the variables within each group—it tells us that an increases in unemployment will increase the probability that a given strike is defensive; it doesn't allow us to conclude, however, that more defensive strikes will occur during negotiations as unemployment increases. Discriminant analysis weighs each variable in order to maximize the separation between defensive and aggressive strikes, irregardless of the number of cases in each group and irrespective of the dynamics within each group. Put simply, discriminant analysis is concerned with maximizing the ratio of between-groups sum of squares to within-groups sum of squares while the probit analysis is concerned only with exploring the resulting within-groups sum of squares. Some variables, therefore, like UM, are good discriminators, with high values successfully predicting a strike as aggressive, but, when used to analyze strike incidence, show that increases in UM actually decrease aggressive strike incidence. Statistically, then, it makes sense to follow a discriminant analysis with a probit analysis since the latter discloses new information not gleaned from the former.

NOTES

1. I have also dropped Gramm's dummy variable indicating that the negotiation is subject to the steel industry's Experimental Negotiating agreement because my data set doesn't include any observations that are affected by the agreement.

2. For reasons not fully understood or explored, union level studies have shown that strike activity is very seasonal (See Kapsa, 1991, Kennan, 1986). If workers know in advance the seasonal fluctuations in demand for a company's product, it serves their interests to time their aggressive and defensive strikes during such periods—baseball players should strike in fall, for instance, during peak demand generated by the playoffs.

3. It is interesting to note that NS and LC might act as proxies for the most unionized sectors in the economy to the extent that they reflect the

relatively more unionized 'core' sector (Edwards, 1979). It would then not surprising that we find these variable significantly contributing to aggressive strike activity.

4. The correlation coefficient between PW and HI is .26 and the correlation between UW and LC is .20.

5. Given an interactive model with the following form:

$$Y = \beta_1 + \beta_2 X_2 + \beta_3 X_3 + \beta_4 (X_2 X_3) + \epsilon$$

the effect of X2 on Y depends on the level of X3. If _4 is positive, the effect of X2 on Y increases as the value of X3 increases (Pindyck and Rubinfeld, 1981, p.110).

6. This is a general test for a nested hypothesis in the context of maximum likelihood estimation. According to Aldrich and Nelson (1988), the general form of the statistic is to take the negative of twice the natural logarithm of the ratio of the two likelihood values (usually reported by the statistical program):

c = -2(log[L0/L1]) = (-2logL0)-(-2L1) = -2(logL0-logL1)

LO is the maximal value of the likelihood function when the constraints implied by the null hypothesis are in force (the coefficients of the variables in question are zero), and L1 is the maximal value under the alternative hypothesis (the likelihood function is estimated without the constraints). If the null hypothesis is true, then the C statistic will follow a chi-squared distribution with the degrees of freedom determined by the number of constraints imposed in the null hypothesis.

7. Gordon, Edwards and Reich (1982) suggest that the new system of labor management that emerged after World-War II involved to a large extent an accord between large firms with market power and large industrial unions, like GM and UAW. They show that large "core firms" with market power are more unionized than smaller, more competitive "peripheral firms" (1982, p. 199).

CHAPTER VII

Conclusion

One main purpose of this book was to identify some important socio-economic determinants of strike activity in the U.S. in the 1970s. It is hoped that this is partially achieved with an alternative framework that analyses strikes in a micro-level econometric study of the historical changes and fluctuations of labor-management relations.

I contend that strike activity in the 1970s can only be approached with an analysis that seriously considers the behavior of both labor and management in their inherent struggle within the workplace. In order fully to capture the behavior of both labor and management, I have divided strikes into two categories: aggressive and defensive. Empirical evidence presented here suggests that these two types of strikes occur under conditions that reflect different degrees of relative power between labor and management. Defensive strikes seem to occur when labor is economically vulnerable to management aggression; aggressive strikes seem to occur when labor is in a better position to exact costs on management.

The majority of strike studies analyze all strikes together. However, these approaches generally lead to inconclusive empirical results and together, over the years, have led to contradictory conclusions. In this presentation, I try to move beyond the earlier literature with an examination of both parties and I specifically try to account for the opposing effects of some variables on the union's and employer's propensity to strike. The analysis presented here suggests that any specification that makes sense of these opposing tendencies must acknowledge the particular historical institutionalization of the balance of power between labor and capital.

Several avenues of future research are suggested by this study. Clearly, more work is necessary at a disaggregated level of analysis. Many variables used here were collected at an aggregate level, like the injury rate, while other variables were only estimates, like the state unemployment rate. An update of the data to include the 1980s would also be desirable. Unfortunately, the BLS stopped collecting strike data for strikes with less than 1,000 workers in 1981. However, work in recent years has filled some gaps and could be used to extend my analysis.[1] Finally, an analysis that investigates the outcomes of defensive and aggressive strikes could shed light on the effectiveness of these types of strikes on wages and working conditions.

Developments in recent years make strike studies even more urgent than ever before. The balance of power between labor and management has shifted dramatically as management has attacked labor through the use of permanent replacement workers during strikes. As a result, labor has lost one of its main sources of strength and power. Strike activity has declined precipitously as unions have assumed a defensive posture, struggling to maintain old, accustomed prerogatives. At the same time, workers have seen their living standards erode.

Originally presented by David Gordon (1996), Figure 6 reproduces the postwar fluctuations in the level of real hourly spendable earnings for private nonfarm production employees. The 1970s mark a clear break as the rapid gains of the 1960s and early 1970s began to fluctuate through the late 1970s. Indeed, these fluctuations reflect a decade of discord, during which labor and capital struggled to reconstitute the terms of their institutional relationship. By the early 1980s, the breakdown of the capital-labor accord resulted in a shift in management's attention away from collective bargaining to an assault on organized labor. In the face of this assault, embodied in the real threat of permanent replacements, workers in the 1980s were powerless to change the long, slow decline in their living standards. Management demanded givebacks in wages and benefits, insisted on the introduction of two-tier wage systems and abandoned employment security by turning to non-union subcontractors and part-time, contingent workers.

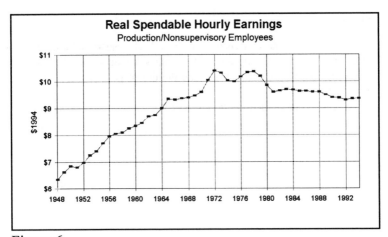

Figure 6.
Source: Gordon (1996), p. 19.

By 1994, real spendable hourly earnings had fallen back to 1967 levels. Real hourly take-home pay was four cents less in 1994 than 1967. During the same time, the economy's real gross output per capita grew 53 percent.

Robert Reich, former Secretary of Labor under the Clinton administration, has argued that business in this time period violated an unwritten "social contract": [2]

> The most important part of the contract is that if the worker is diligent and reliable, and if the company is making money, that worker keeps his or her job. The second principle is enjoying rising wages and benefits as a company's profits improve. This social contract is no longer with us. (Bearak, 1995, p. A10).

The time is long overdue to begin building new structures of labor-management relations based on mutual respect, fairness and democracy in the workplace. A good start would be a ban on the use of striker replacements so that workers could begin to recover some of their basic rights and past prerogatives in the workplace.

NOTES

1. The U.S. General Accounting office (GAO) constructed a database of strikes in 1985 and 1989 in response to Congress's request for information for documentation of "trends in strikes and the use of permanent replacements" (1991, p.9).

2. Quoted in Gordon (1996, pp. 64-65).

Appendix

In this appendix, I define and provide source documentation for all the variables used in the discriminant and probit procedures outlined above. I use the following abbreviations: CPS, Current Population Survey; BLS, Bureau of Labor Statistics; BNA, Bureau of National Affairs; and SCB, Survey of Current Business.

Strike Data

Two sources provide the raw data for strike activity: the discriminant analysis relies on strike data collected by the Bureau of Labor Statistics, U.S. Department of Labor and the probit analysis uses a comprehensive sample of contract negotiations collected by Cynthia Gramm.

The BLS strike data documents every strike in the 1970s that includes three or more workers. Each strike observation includes a number of important details: major issue, state and three digit standard industrial code. These data allowed me to classify 110 strikes by their major issue and another 8,000 with the discriminant procedure. I then matched 120 of these classified strikes to Cynthia Gramm's data set.

This data set, generously provided by Cynthia Gramm, is derived from a single comprehensive sample of 6,046 contract negotiations occurring in 1971-80 in bargaining units of 1,000 or more workers. As Gramm states, this data set is superior to those used in previous studies because it measures strike probabilities (or propensities) directly rather than by proxy. The sample of contract negotiations was obtained from 1971-1980 issues of the U.S. Bureau of Labor statistics' *Bargaining Calendar* and *Wage Calendar*. Gramm matched information in these annual bulletins with strike information from two weekly pamphlets published by the BLS: *Industrial Relations Facts* and *Current Work Stoppages*, producing a single micro-level sample of negotiations in which strike incidence is observed. I used these data to conduct two separate probit estimations of 868 collective bargaining negotiations between 1971-80: one estimation for 62 defensive strikes and another for 58 aggressive strikes.

Two words of caution are in order concerning Gramm's data set. First, strike probabilities in the set can be unbiased only if the negotiations in the sample are independent. However, for some months, unions and industries, this independence assumption may be invalid. This may be the case for industries or unions in which, although several separate contracts result, several bargaining units negotiate jointly or in close coordination. Secondly, there is evidence that a sample of strikes with a thousand or more workers is not representative of all strikes. According to Skeels (1988), strike samples of a thousand or more workers in the 1980s do not appear to meet the basic requirement of randomness because bargaining unit size has a systematic relationship to contract status, geographic distribution and industry. Simply put, small strikes are different than large ones. For Skeels, although coefficient signs in regressions are consistent for strikes of different sizes, their significance levels are unreliable. For this reason, the results of the probit analysis of Gramm's data should be interpreted as representative of strikes that only include a thousand or more workers.

Capitalist Strength

State Unemployment Rate (UN)

Because monthly state and regional unemployment rates are unavailable, Cynthia Gramm estimates the unemployment rate in the state or region in which the bargaining unit is located in the following manner:

$$Ue_{sm} = (UE_{sy}/UE_{fy})*UE_{fm}$$

where s denotes state or region, f denotes national, m denotes the month, y denotes the year and UE denotes unemployment as a percent of the adult civilian labor force. Of course the approach assumes that the ratio of the yearly state unemployment rate to the yearly national unemployment rate remains the same for every month of the year.

Injury Rates (INJ)

The annual injury rate at the level of 2-digit SIC manufacturing industries is based on data collected by the BLS. However, one drawback to the data is that in 1971, after the creation of OSHA, the BLS changed its method for collecting and calculating the injury rate, thereby creating two discontinuous time series for the 1970s. To assure maximum consistency between the two series I followed the "splicing" method described by Peter Arno (1982). According to this method, new and consistent values for 1971 through 1980 are calculated with the ratio between the predicted value and actual value for 1971. In other words, the new "spliced" series is defined as:

$$INJ_s i = INJ_n i * (INJ_o 71 / INJ_n 71)$$

where I = 1972....1980, INJ_o is the old BLS injury rate series from 1940 to 1970, INJ_n is the new injury rate series for the years from 1971 to the present, and $INJ_o 71$ is an expected value for 1971 that was projected from the old series using an ordinary least squares regression equation for the years 1948-1970. For all two digit industries, I used the following specification of the old injury rate to forecast the value for 1971:

$$INJ_o{}^i = \alpha_i + \beta_1 P_i + \beta_2 O_i + \beta_3 K_i + \beta_4 D_i + \beta_5 Y_i + \beta_6 t_i\, \beta_7 t^2{}_i + \mu_i$$

where the variables are defined as follows:

P = after-tax corporate rate

O = average weekly hours of overtime by production workers

K = utilized stock of manufacturing equipment per production worker hour

D = percentage of manufacturing equipment 10-19 years old

Y = proportion of male production workers aged 18-34 in civilian labor force

This specification is a rather robust predictor of the postwar injury rate and, as shown by Peter Arno, creates a strong foundation for establishing a continuous series for two digit industries in the 1970s.

Unfair Labor Practices (UF)

UF, a measure of unfair labor practices, is defined as the ratio of the annual section 8(A) charges received by the National Labor Relations Board to the number of unionized workers for the year in the two digit industry. Section 8(A) charges are published in the *Annual Report of the National Relations Board*. Most section 8(A) charges are filed for alleged violations of subsections 8(A)(3) and 8(A)(5) of the *National Labor Relations Act* of 1935. Section 8(A)(3) states that "it shall be an unfair labor practice for an employer...by discrimination in regard to hire or tenure of employment or condition of employment to encourage or discourage membership in any labor organization", while section 8(A)(5) states that "it shall be an unfair labor practice for an employer...to refuse to bargain collectively with representatives of his employees..." I collected data on the number of unionized workers in an industry from the Annual CPS tapes.

Workers' Strength

State Unionization Rate (SU)

Freeman and Medoff (1979) estimate unionization by state grouping from weighted counts of employed private sector wage and salary workers on the 1973-75 May CPS tapes according to the formula:

$$M_{jk} = (\Sigma \, \delta_{ijk} \, \omega_{ijk} / \Sigma \, \omega_{ijk}) * 100$$

where M_{jk} is the percentage of workers in group k in state group j who are union members, with K indexing production or non-production workers,

δ_{ijk} is a dichotomous variable string whether employee I is a union member ($\delta_{ijk}=1$) or not ($\delta_{ijk}=0$) and,

ω_{ink} is the CPS sampling weight attached to employee I.

These estimates are limited to 29 state groups used in the CPS surveys. Unfortunately, this procedure ignores small, highly unionized states, such as West Virginia, because they are grouped with low unionization states, like South Carolina. This may explain some of the weak results on the significance level for defensive strikes. Additionally, it should be noted that a higher percentage of employed private-sector wage-and-salary workers might have been members of unions than indicated on the CPS tapes. Other estimates provided to the BLS, based on EEG (Expenditures for Employee Compensation) and union surveys, show higher unionization rates; the unions reported a 1974 membership equal to 28.5 percent , whereas the CPS projects only 22.6 % of the relevant workforce (Freeman and Medoff, 1979, p. 171).

Discrimination (PM), (PW), (UW), (UM)

The following details the procedures I used to estimate the relative wage rate by race and gender for full time, unionized wage workers for 1971-1980. These estimates were calculated for 3 digit 1970 census industries. Data on union organization of the work force and detailed information on personal characteristics is provided by the Current Population Survey conducted by the BLS. Since May 1973, the May CPS questionnaire has enquired about the union status of each individual who is in the labor force, asking "does ...belong to a labor union?" In addition, the survey asked for the wage rate of full-time workers. One drawback of this survey is that the union question relates to membership rather than coverage by a union-management agreement. As Freeman and Medoff have pointed out, the effect of collective bargaining is likely to be misstated if a significant number of nonmembers are covered by contracts or if a significant number of members are not covered.

Following Freeman and Medoff, I pooled the data in order to obtain a reliable number of observations. Data form the 1973-76 May CPS reports was first pooled, followed by the 1977-80 reports. Because the data begin only in 1973, I used the results from the first period to cover the years 1971-76. This procedure, along with the pooling, may mask inter-year differences, but since relative wages change very little over such small time periods, any bias should be minimal (Freeman and Medoff estimate that the percentage unionized for the United States fell only 2.4% between 1970 and 1974).

I calculated relative wages, UM and UW, according to the following formulas:

$$UM_{jk} = ((\Sigma MW_{jki}{}^* \mu_{jki})/\Sigma \mu_{jki})/((\Sigma FW_{jkf}{}^* \mu_{jki})/\Sigma \mu_{jki})$$

$$UW_{jk} = ((\Sigma WW_{jki}{}^* \mu_{jki})/\Sigma \mu_{jki})/((\Sigma BW_{jki}{}^* \mu_{jki})/\Sigma \mu_{jki})$$

where UM_{jk} is the relative wage rate of males to females for unionized workers in pool k in industry j and UW_{jk} is the relative wage rate of white to nonwhites for unionized workers in pool k in industry j,
MW is the wage rate for male individual I and FW is the wage rate for female individual I,
WW is the wage rate for white individual I and BW is the wage rate for non-white individual I,
and
μ_{jki} is the CPS sampling weight attached to employee I.

In a similar fashion, the proportion of unionized workers in the unit's industry who are male and the proportion who are white was also taken from the CPS tapes and pooled for the two time periods, 1973-1976 and 1977-1980.

Relative Quits (QL)

This variable is defined as the ratio of quits to layoffs for individual three digit industries. The data come from BLS *Employment and Earnings, United States 1908-1978 and updated in annual issue of Employment and Earnings* for the remaining years. Data on disk were provided by Bruce Pietrykowski.

Workers' Expectations

Index of Workers' Expectations (EXP)

Workers' expectations are defined as the ratio of the percentage change in nominal wages (straight plus COLA) of janitors or laborers to the percentage change in the consumer price index over the term of the previous contract. The variable pertaining to the terms of the wages over the previous contract was collected directly from contracts on file at the BLS or public sources, including issues of *Daily Labor Reports* (BNA), *Current Wage Developments* (BLS) and *Wage Chronicles* (BLS). This variable, along with changes in the CPI over the previous contract, was collected by Wallace Hendricks and Lawrence Kahn and provided by Cynthia Gramm.

Capitalist Economic Vulnerability

Variation in Shipments (SH)

This measure is defined as the intrayear coefficient of variation in shipments in the unit's industry for the year preceding the negotiation. It was computed from the Bureau of Census, *Manufacturers' Shipments, Inventories and Orders* (M3-1.11), 1958-1981 and was generously provided by Cynthia Gramm.

Change in New Orders (PN), (NO)

Quarterly and annual data on new orders was collected form the same source as data on shipments: Bureau of the Census, *Manufacturers' Shipments, Inventories and Orders* (M3-1.11), 1958-1981. On the basis of these data. two variables were constructed:

 PN: the percentage change in new orders received by the unit's industry over the year ending the month preceding negotiations;
 NO: the percent of the previous years' new orders in the unit's industry that was received during the quarter ending the month preceding the negotiations.

Both variables were provided by Cynthia Gramm.

Ratio of Labor Costs to Value Added (LC)

This is defined as the ratio of labor costs to value added at the two digit industrial level. Data were collected from the CPS annual tapes.

Industry Workers who are Non-Supervisory (NS)

This is defined as the percent of workers in the unit's three digit industry who are employed in nonsupervisory production and service occupations. Obtained from BLS, CPS tapes.

Workers' Economic Vulnerability

Cost of Job Loss (CJL)

The cost of job loss has been estimated and used to explain the aggregate slowdown in U.S. productivity growth (Weisskopf, Bowles and Gordon, 1983) and profitability (Bowles, Gordon and Weisskopf, 1986). In an article in 1983, Bowles and Schor successfully used the cost of job loss as a measure of relative worker power in explaining strike activity. All of these studies employ the following formulation in order to measure the cost of job loss:

$$w - [u_d w_s + (1 - u_d)w_n]$$

where u_d is a measure of the average duration of unemployment for workers who lose their jobs; w represents the average weekly after-tax wage for production workers; w_s is a measure of the average weekly income-replacing benefits; and w_n is the average expected annual reemployment earnings. The cost of job loss is the difference between current earnings and an average of expected future earnings and the income-replacing social welfare benefit, weighted by the expected duration of unemployment. I utilize the annual percentage change in the cost of job loss at the three digit SIC level to measure working class economic vulnerability and the ensuing balance of power between workers and management. Unfortunately, the CJL is not able entirely to provide an industry-specific calculation of the actual cost of loosing your job because the unemployment rate is not available in disaggregated form; only national figures are available. This variable was generously provided by Thomas Weisskopf.

Controls

Business Cycle (BC)

Business cycle peak and trough years are identified by looking at levels of capacity utilization for the domestic private non-residential economy. Method and data are presented in Peter Clark (1979). Clark estimates potential output by applying the method used by Council of Economic Advisors - a method that estimates the ratio of actual gross national product to the corresponding potential GNP. By this measure there were two business cycle peaks in the 1970s (1973 and 1979) and two troughs (1971 and 1975). In this book, I control for the business cycle with a dummy variable, BC, that takes on a value of 1 for the downswing and 0 for the upswing.

Wage-Price Controls (C)

This dummy variable has fractional values as well as positive and negative values. Fractional values correspond to years when the wage-price controls were in effect for only for a few months, and the negative numbers capture "catch-up" effects that operated in the period following the end of the wage-price controls (See R.J. Gordon, 1982). Specifically: 1971=.25; 1972-73=1; 1974-75=-1; elsewhere=0.

8-Firm Concentration Ratio (HC)

Constructed as a dummy variable indicating that the eight firm concentration ratio in the unit's industry is greater than 70%. Obtained from the U.S. Department of Commerce *1972 Census of Manufacturers*.

[illegible] the [illegible] rate [illegible] not available [illegible]
this [illegible] only national figures are available [illegible] the variable
was [illegible] provided by Thomas Weisskopf.

Controls

[illegible]

[illegible] and [illegible] levels [illegible] private and residential [illegible] Clark [illegible] Controls [illegible] total gross [illegible] this measure [illegible] 1972 and 1987 [illegible] business [illegible] and [illegible]

[illegible]

[illegible] positive and [illegible] when the [illegible] and the [illegible]

[illegible]

[illegible]

Bibliography

Arno, Peter, "The Political Economy of Industrial Injuries." Ph.D dissertation, New School for Social Research, 1984.

Ashenfelter, Orley and George E. Johnson, "Bargaining Theory, Trade Unions and Industrial Strike Activity." *American Economic Review* (May 1969).

Bell, Daniel, *The End Of Ideology.* Glencoe, Ill: Free Press, 1960.

Bluestone, Barry and Harrison, Bennett, *The Deindustrialization of America.* New York: Basic Books, 1982.

Bornstein, Stephen, Held, David and Krieger, Joel (eds), *The State in Capitalist Europe.* London: George Allen & Unwin, 1984.

Bornstein, Stephen, "States and unions: from postwar settlement to contemporary stalemate", in S. Bornstein, D. Held and J. Krieger eds, *The State in Capitalist Europe.* London: George Allen & Unwin, 1984.

Bowles, Samuel, Thomas E. Weisskopf, David M. Gordon, *Beyond the Wasteland.* New York: Anchor Press, 1984.

Bowles, Sam and Edwards, Richard, *Understanding Capitalism.* New York: Harper and Row: 1985.

Braverman, Harry, *Labor and Monopoly Capital: The Degradation of Work in the Twentieth Century* New York: Monthly Review Press, 1974.

Brenner, Robert, "The Origins of Capitalist Development: A Critique of Neo-Smithean Marxism." *New Left Review* (July-August 1977).

Brody, David, *Workers in Industrial America.* Oxford: Oxford University Press, 1980.

Burawoy, Michael, "Between the Labor Process and the State: The Changing Face of Factory Regimes Under Advanced Capitalism." *American Sociological Review* 48 (October 1983).

Burawoy, Michael, *The Politics of Production.* London: Verso, 1985.

Bureau of National Affairs, Inc., *Collective Bargaining Negotiations and Contracts. Basic Patterns in Union Contracts. Vol. 2: Management and Union Rights* Washington, D.C.: BNA, Inc., 1986.

Byrne, Dennis M. and Randall H. King, "Wildcat Strikes in U.S. Manufacturing, 1960-1977." *Journal of Labor Research* 7 (Fall 1986).

Cameron, David R., "Corporatism, Labor Quiescence and the Representation of Economic Interest in Advanced Capitalist Society," in John H. Goldthorpe (ed) *Order and Conflict in Contemporary Capitalism*. New York: Oxford University Press, 1985.

Christiansen, Jens, *Labour Productivity in the Steel Industry: A Comparative Study of the Federal Republic of Germany and the United States of America*. Ph.D. dissertation, Stanford University, 1983.

Cohen, Stephen S. and John Zysman, *Manufacturing Matters*. New York: Basic Books, 1987.

Commons, John, *Institutional Economics*. New York: Macmillan, 1934.

Doeringer, Peter and Piore, Michael, *Internal Labor Markets and Manpower Analysis*. Lexington, MA: D.C. Heath, 1970.

Dunlop, John T., "Have the 1980s changed U.S. industrial relations?" *Monthly Labor Review* (May 1988).

Edwards, P.K., "Time Series Regression Models of Strike Activity: A Reconsideration with American Data." *British Journal of Indusrial Relations* (Nov. 1978).

Edwards, Richard, *Contested Terrain*. New York: Basic Books, 1979.

Engels, "Socialism: Utopian and Scientific," in Robert C. Tucker, *The Marx-Engels Reader*. New York: Norton & Company, 1978.

Erbes-Seguin, Sabine, "Trade unions, Employers and the State: toward a new relationship?" in Mark Kesselman (ed) *The French Workers' Movement: Economic Crisis and Political Change*. London: George Allen & Unwin, 1984.

Farber, H.S., "Bargaining Theory, Wage Outcomes and the Occurrence of Strikes." *American Economic Review* (June 1978).

Flaherty, Sean, "Contract Status and the Economic Determinants of Strike Activity." *Industrial Relations*, (Winter 1983).

Flaherty, Sean, "Strike Activity, Worker Militancy and Productivity Change in the United States Manufacturing Sector." Mimeographed paper, Department of Economics, Franklin and Marshall College (1986).

Flaherty, Sean, "Mature Collective Bargaining and Rank and File Militlancy: Breaking the Peace of the "Treaty of Detroit." Mimeographed paper, Department of Economics, Franklin and Marshall College (1986).

Foner, Phillip, *Organized Labor and the Black Worker Freeman, 1619-1973.* New York: Praeger, 1974.

Franzosi, Robert, "One Hundred Years of Strike Statistics: Methodological and Theoretical Issues in Quantitative Strike Research." *Industrial and Labor Relations Review* 42.

Freedman, Audrey, "How the 1980s have changed industrial relations." *Monthly Labor Review* (May 1988).

Goldthorpe, John H., (ed) *Order and Conflict in Contemporary Capitalism.* New York: Oxford University Press, 1985.

Goldthorpe, John D., "The End of Convergence: Corporatism and Dualism in Modern Western Societies", in John H. Goldthorpe (ed), *Order and Conflict in Contemporary Capitalism: Studies in the Political Economy of Western European Nations.* Oxford: Clarendon Press, 1984.

Gordon, David M., Edwards, Richard and Reich, Michael, *Segmented Work, Divided Workers: The Historical Transformation of Labor in the United States.* New York: Cambridge University Press, 1982.

Gordon, David M., "The Best Defense is a Good Defense: Toward a Marxian Theory of Labor Union Structure and Behavior," in M.Carte and W. Leahy, eds., *New Directions in Labor Economics and Industrial Relations*, Notre Dame Press, 1981.

Gordon, David M., *Fat and Mean,* New York: The Free Press, 1996.

Gordon, Robert J., "A Century of Evidence on Wage and Price Stickiness in the United States, the United Kingdom and Japan," in James Tobin, ed., *Macroeconomics, Prices and Quantities*, Washington D.C.: Brookings Institution, 1982.

Gramm, Cynthia L., "New Measures of the Propensity to Strike During Contract Negotiations, 1971-1980. *Industrial and Labor Relations Review* 40 (April 1987).

Gramm, Cynthia L., "Strike Incidence and Severity: A Micro Level Study." *Industrial and Labor Relations Review* 39 (April, 1986).

Griffin, John I., *Strikes: A Study in Quantitative Economics.* New York: Columbia University Press, 1939.

Hibbs, Douglas A. Jr., "Industrial conflict in advanced industrial societies", *American Political Science Review* (December 1976).

Hicks, J., *The Theory of Wages.* Macmillan: New York, 1932.

Hill, Stephen, *Competition and Control at Work: New Industrial Sociology.* Cambridge: MIT Press, 1981.

Hogan, Lloyd, *Principles of Black Political Economy.* New York: Routledge and Kegan Paul, 1984.

Hyman, Richard, *Industrial Relations: A Marxist Introduction.* MacMillan, London, 1975.

Hyman, Richard and Elger, Tony, "Job Controls, the Employers' Offensive, and Alternative Strategies", *Capital and Class* 15 (Autumn 1981).

Kaufman, Bruce E., "Bargaining Theory, Inflation, and Cyclical Strike Activity in Manufacturing." *Industrial and Labor Relations Review* 34 (April 1981).

Kaufman, Bruce E., "The Determinants of Strikes, 1900-1977." *Industrial and Labor Relations Review* 35 (July 1982).

Kennan, John, "The Economics of Strikes," in O. Ashenfelter and R. Layard, eds., *Handbook of Labor Economics, Volume II,* New York: Elsevier Science Publishers, 1986.

Kennan, John, "Pareto Optimality and the Economics of Strike Duration," *Journal of Labor Research* 1 (Spring 1982).

Kochan, Thomas A., Harry C. Katz, and Nancy R. Mower, *Worker Participation and American Unions.* Kalamazoo, MI: W.E. Upjohn Institute for Employment Research, 1984.

Kochan, Thomas, and Piore, Michael, "U.S. Industrial Relations in Transition", in Thomas Kochan (ed), *Challenges and Choices Facing American Labor.* Cambridge: MIT Press, 1985.

Korpi, Walter and Michael Shalev, "Strikes, Industrial Relations and Class Conflict in Capitalist Societies" *British Journal of Sociology* 30 (1979).

Korpi, Walter, *The Working Class in Welfare Capitalism: Work, Unions and Politics in Sweden.* London: Routledge, 1978.

Lipset, Seymour M. (ed), *Unions in Transition: Entering the Second Century.* San Francisco: Institute for Contemporary Studies, 1986.

Lipsky, David B. and Clifford B. Donn (eds), *Collective Bargaining in American Industry.* New York: Lexington Books, 1987.

Maki, Dennis R., "The Effect of Strikes on the Volume of Strike Activity." *Industrial and Labor Relations Review* 39 (July 1986).

Marglin, Stephen A., "Catching Flies with Honey: An Inquiry into Management Initiatives to Humanize Work" *Economic Analysis and Workers' Management* 11 (1979).

Marx, Karl, *Capital, Vol. I.* New York: International Publishers, 1967.

Mauro, Martin J., "Strikes as a Result of Imperfect Information." *Industrial and Labor Relations Review* 35 (July 1982).

Montgomery, David. *Workers' Control in America.* Cambridge: Cambridge University Press, 1979.

Naples, Michele I., "An Analysis of Defensive Strikes." *Industrial Relations* 26 (Winter 1987).

Naples, Michele I., "Production is a Human Activity: A Social Relations Approach to the Productivity Slowdown." Unpublished paper.

Naples, Michele I., "Industrial Conflict and Its Implications for Productivity Growth." *American Economic Review, Papers and Proceedings* LXXI (May 1981).

Naples, Michele I., "The Unraveling of the Union-Capital Truce and the U.S. Industrial Productivity Crisis." *Review of Radical Political Economy* XVII (Spring/Summer 1986).

National Labor Relations Board, *Legislative History of the National Labor Relations Act, 1935.* Washington: GPO, 1985.

National Labor Relations Act, June 29 1935, c. 49 Stat. 449 (1935).

Neumann, George R. and Melvin W. Reder, "Conflict and Contract: The Case of Strikes." *Journal of Political Economy* 88 (October).

Neumann, George R. and Melvin W. Reder, "Output and Strike Activity in U.S. Manufacturing: How Large are the Losses?" *Industrial and Labor Relations Review* 37 (Jan. 1984).

Paldam, Martin and Peder Pederson, "The Macroeconomic Strike Model: A Study of Seventeen Countries, 1948-1975." *Industrial and Labor Relations Review* 35 (July 1982).

Panitch, Leo, "Trade Unions and the Capitalist State." *New Left Review* 123 (January 1981).

Panitch, Leo, *Working Class Politics in Crisis: Essays on Labour and the State.* London: Verso, 1986.

Parker, Mike, *Inside the Circle* Boston: South End Press, 1985.

Parsley, C.J., "Labor Union Effects on Wage Gains: A Survey Of Recent Literature." *Journal of Economic Literature* 18 (March 1980).

Pignon D. and Querzola J., "Dictatorship and Democracy in Production", in Andre Gorz (ed), *The Division of Labour.* Brighton: Harvester Press, 1976.

Pindyck, Robert and Rubinfield, Daniel, *Econometric Models and Economic Forecasts.* New York: McGraw-Hill, 1981.

Piore, Michael J., "The Technological Foundations of Dualism and discontinuity", in Suzanne Berger and Michael J. Piore (eds), *Dualism and Discountinuity in Industrial Societies.* Cambridge: Cambridge University Press, 1980.

Piore, Michael J. and Sabel, Charles F., *The Second Industrial Divide.* New York: Basic Books, 1984.

Przeworski, Adam, *Capitalism and Social Democracy.* Cambridge: Cambridge University Press, 1986.

Przeworski, Adam "Social Democracy as a Historical Phenomenon." *New Left Review* 122 (August 1980).

Rees,A. "Industrial Conflict and Business Fluctuations" *Journal of Political Economy* LX (1952).

Richard B. and James L. Medoff, *What Do Unions Do?* New York: Basic Books, 1984.

Sabel, Charles F., "A Fighting Chance: Structural Change and New Labor Strategies." *International Journal of Political Economy* (Fall 1987).

Schor, Juliet B. and Samuel Bowles, "The Cost of Job Loss and the Incidence of Strikes." Unpublished, University of Massachusetts, Amherst.

Shalev, Michael, "Trade Unionism and Economic Analysis: The Case of Industrial Conflict." *Journal of Labor Research* 1 (Spring 1980).

Skeels, Jack W, "Measures of U.S. Strike Activity." *Industrial and Labor Relations Review* 35 (no. 24).

Snyder, David, "Early North American Strikes: A Reinterpretation." *Industrial and Labor Relations Review* 30 (April 1977).

Stern, Robert N., "Methodological Issues in Quantitative Strike Analysis." *Industrial Relations* 17 (Feb. 1978)

Tracy, Joseph S, "An Empirical Test of an Asymmetric Information Model of Strikes." *Journal of Labor Economics* 5 (no. 2).

United States General Accounting Office, Human Resources Division, *Labor-Management Relations: Strikes and the Use of Permanent Strike Replacements in the 1970s and 1980s*, GAO/HRD-91-1, January 19, 1991.

Weisskopf, Thomas, David M. Gordon, and Samuel Bowles, "Hearts and Minds: A Social Model of U.S. Productivity Growth," *Brookings Papers on Economic Activity* 2 (1983).

Wheeler, Hoyt et. al., "Determinants of Strikes: Comment." *Industrial and Labor Relations Review* 37 (January 1984).

Wood, Stephen (ed), *The Degradation of Work?* London: Hutchinson & Co., 1982.

Zimbalist, Andrew (ed), *Case Studies on the Labor Process.* New York: Monthly Review Press, 1979.

Index

DATE DUE

DEMCO, INC. 38-2931